D1156016

THE ELEMENTS OF LETTERING

THE ELEMENTS OF LETTERING

BY
JOHN HOWARD BENSON
AND
ARTHUR GRAHAM CAREY

NEW YORK   TORONTO   LONDON
McGRAW–HILL BOOK COMPANY, INC.
1950

72727

DEDICATED TO

ESTHER FISHER BENSON AND ELISABETH FOSTER CAREY

OUR PATIENT WIVES

CONTENTS

CONTENTS

BOOK THREE. THE HISTORICAL ELEMENTS

PART A. THE ANCIENT WORLD

PART B. THE MEDIEVAL WORLD

PART C. THE MODERN WORLD

FOREWORD

THE purpose of this treatise is entirely practical. It aims to help to a better practice of lettering those who are interested. Though the first book is theoretical, and the last historical, these exist merely as aids to the discussion of practice between them. We put the theoretical book first because we cannot do anything until we know what to do; and the historical book last because when we have done something, it is useful to see how other people have done similar things. It is useless to try to find out how other people have solved their problems, when, through lack of practical experience, we do not yet know what such problems are.

Each of these books tries to reduce a vast amount of particular fact to a statement which is useful because understandable, and understandable because simple. It is not possible to achieve this without over-simplification. But a treatise which, to avoid over-simplification, examined every exceptional case—theoretical, practical, and historical—would need an army of encyclopedists to write it, and a student with many otherwise unoccupied years to read it. Bad as this would be, it would be worse to write a treatise that sacrificed truth to convenience, and to produce something easy to read, but worthless when read. We, therefore, begin each book with the simplest discoverable elements of lettering from the point of view of that book. We try to continue each as a reasonable development from those simplicities. And so we hope that our simplifications are not arbitrary patterns violently imposed upon the facts, but indications of the main truths of our subject. If we have succeeded in stating clearly the more general truths, we need not be disturbed if exceptions are found. We are not concerned with exceptions, but with principles. A map which limits itself to the statement of a few important geographical facts is as true as one not so limited, and it is better because more useful to those who would find their way.

BOOK ONE

THE THEORETICAL ELEMENTS
OR
LETTERS AS THINGS TO BE UNDERSTOOD

PART A. THE GENERAL PROBLEM

PART B. THE PARTICULAR PROBLEM

PART C. THE PROBLEM OF WORK

THE THEORETICAL ELEMENTS
OR
LETTERS AS THINGS TO BE UNDERSTOOD

PART A. THE GENERAL PROBLEM

1. ART. Lettering is an art. Art is a department of human activity concerning which there is such widespread confusion today that before attempting to understand the particular art of making letters, we must first consider the nature of art in general. According to the dictionary, art is the skillful making of things by human beings. This is the original and basic meaning of the word. It has been expanded thus: Art is the imposition of a Mental Image upon Material, by certain Means, for a given End.

2. PURPOSE. This end or purpose of a thing to be made is the first concern of the intelligent artist. The object must be thought of from the point of view of its user, its consumer, the patron. Nothing is made by art unless some person desires good as a result of that making, and this good is one of the thing's causes. To understand the thing you must appreciate this reason for its existence. You cannot know what it is unless you know what good it is. The maker cannot make well unless he knows and respects function.

3. MATERIAL. The artist does not create his materials, but chooses from all the kinds already in existence. All materials have their own qualities and qualifications. Each kind—marble, bronze, wood, or paint—has laws of its own which demand considerate treatment at the artist's hands. You cannot expect to produce good works if you treat your materials without reference to their nature. You can make things skillfully only if you know the possibilities of your chosen material, and respect and cooperate with these possibilities. Proper use of material means knowledge of it, and a willingness to work with and not against what is known.

4. TOOLS. Materials are shaped in many different ways—by cutting, modelling, melting, hammering, weaving. The handling of every kind of material depends upon physical forces that obey natural

3

laws. The application of almost all these forces involves the use of tools and instruments. These tools, and the physical laws that are behind their use, must be known and respected by the craftsman. Proper handling of material means knowledge of the tools by which it is shaped, and a willingness to use these according to their natures rather than in violation of them.

5. IMAGE. An object of art differs from an object of nature because it is the product of a human mind. The imagination is itself an instrument and, like others, it marks its product with qualities that are its own. Images produced in an artist's imagination have a quality which results from their origin. The objects which are the material copies of these images have that stamp also. The word used to describe this in works of art is the word *formal*. Formal qualities are in general concerned with color and sound relationships, space and line relationships, and with rhythms and harmonies most of which seem to lend themselves to mathematical interpretation.

6. SENSES. The ancient psychologists counted five senses—sight, hearing, smell, taste, and touch. The moderns have added two more —kinaesthesis and stasis. By kinaesthesis we are made aware of what our own muscles are doing. Stasis tells us about our relation to the vertical, and helps us to keep our balance. These seven senses are the means by which human minds make contact with the realities outside them. They bring to the intelligence the only accounts it gets of the great, exterior, objective world.

7. IMAGINATION. Such accounts are the external concern of the senses, but these also have an internal activity which is called the Imagination. When you see pictures in your mind's eye, you are enjoying the inward working of the sense of sight—seeing visual images. Human beings are so dependent on the sense of sight that we sometimes think of the imagination as producing visual images only. But there are images for each sense. The musician hears auditory images in his imagination, and we hear them when we think about music that we have heard before. The cook has gustatory images in her mind, and imposes these upon her materials in the kitchen. The dressmaker and sculptor use tactile images. But just as important are the images resulting from the internal working of the kinaesthetic sense.

4

8. KINAESTHESIS. The kinaesthetic nerves are in the muscles themselves, and can therefore report to the brain what the muscles are doing. If you shut your eyes and describe a *figure eight* in the air, it is a kinaesthetic image that guides your hand. Such images are limited by the nature of the muscular structure concerned, and are therefore patterns of motions that the muscles *are able to make*. But they are also limited by the formalizing nature of the imagination in general, and are therefore definitely *patterns*, often susceptible of mathematical interpretation. All the arts use kinaesthetic images. Dancing is little more than an exercise of this sense. In the drama and in sports their importance is obvious. So also in the art of writing. When you make letters with a pen, the shapes are controlled more by the feeling you have in your hand than by what your eye sees. Your eye keeps the letters on the line and corrects the worst illegibilities; that is about all. Except for such corrections, we can all write with our eyes shut almost as well as with them open.

9. OBJECT AND SUBJECT. The artist can never know too much, nor think too consciously, about the functional and technical parts of his problem. He must keep constantly before him the purpose of the thing he is making, and equally clear the natures of his chosen materials and tools. These things are not by nature part of him, and only become part of his mental equipment by years of practice. But his imagination *is* a natural part of the artist himself—just as truly a part of him as is his digestion. And like the digestion, the imagination works best when properly nourished, and then let alone. By thinking about the working of your imagination, or about the formal part of design, of which the healthy imagination takes care, you will become self-conscious and confused. The best art has always been produced by men who have concentrated upon the objective aspects of their job—function and technique—and who have paid little or no attention to its subjective aspects—imagination and the formal qualities which are its natural effect.

10. ORIGINALITY. When the imagination does not work normally or freely, and does not produce original creative ideas, the designer is forced to copy the shapes of things already in existence. All existent things are either natural objects—rocks, trees, animals—or

5

artificial objects—boats, books, houses. If the shapes he copies are from nature, we call his art Naturalistic. If he copies artificial things, we call it Derivative. His art can be called Original only when all the conditions of the particular job to be done have been freshly organized in his imagination.

11. PERFECTION. A perfect thing is one which is fully itself—as it ought to be, according to its own inner principles. Thus, perfect snow is white, and sooty snow imperfect, because whiteness is an essential of snow. The surface of a perfect sphere is everywhere equidistant from its center, because that is of the nature of spheres. A perfect statue of Apollo carved in stone is a combination of the idea of Apollo, the nature of stone, and the nature of carving—each treated as it should be, and in proper relation to the others. Perfect means *per fectum*, thoroughly made. We have various ways of appreciating the perfection of a thing. We can realize its perfection by wanting to use it, and when this happens, we desire its Goodness. Or we can reason about the thing, and understand its Truth. Or we can wonder at the perfection without desire to use, and without reasoning, and then we admire its Beauty. We have no means of realizing perfection as such, but we have voluntary, rational, and intuitive faculties which open up the perfection of a thing to our minds, under these three aspects.

12. REASON AND INTUITION. The use of will and reason in art is obvious, and the use of the aesthetic intuition is easy to understand. The artist uses all these together, or one after another. He reasons out what he is going to do, and does it. Then he turns the intuitive part of his mind toward the result, and learns that some parts are beautiful and others ugly. He gets to work again with his reason on the ugly parts, corrects the errors, and again submits the result to the aesthetic judgment. In this way, will, reason, and intuition cooperate for the good of the thing to be made.

13. WHOLE AND PARTS. Things are made up of parts, and the parts of a perfect thing are perfect also, and perfectly related to one another. Whether we realize perfection as Goodness, as Truth, or as Beauty, the proposition stands. A thing is not good unless its parts, and their arrangement, contribute to its usefulness. And a true thing

6

is made up of parts which share its genuineness. So also with Beauty. A beautiful thing is made up of admirable parts, admirably arranged. The goodness, the truth, and the beauty of whole things cannot be achieved, if these aspects of perfection are not achieved also in the parts of which they are built.

PART B. THE PARTICULAR PROBLEM

Chapter 1. LETTER IDEAS

1. LETTERING. No art exemplifies these general principles better than does that of lettering. Its purpose is clear—plain legibility. The Materials and Tools are simple, and the effect of their intelligent use upon the writing is immediately obvious. The images of the letters are simple and unified. In no art is the logic and reasonableness of the right use of the four artistic essentials more manifest.

2. GEOMETRIC LETTERS. To understand this logic and reasonableness we must begin at the beginning—with the basic concepts of the letter forms. These may be defined in the language of plane geometry. We notice that Euclid's word στοιχεῖον, which we translate *element*, is also the ordinary Greek word for *letter*. The Greeks so identified letters and geometric elements that they used the same word for both. These geometric letter-ideas are composed of lines, straight and regularly curved. They have no forms that cannot be materialized with a ruler and compasses.

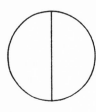

3. GEOMETRIC ELEMENTS. Consider, for a moment, the nature of the elements with which the austere science of geometry deals. Lines are definitions of direction, changing or unchanging. Geometric plane figures are surfaces bounded by lines. Lines have quantity—length and quality—direction. Plane figures also have quantity and quality. The quantity of a plane figure is its area. The quality of a plane figure is its shape, which is defined by the directions of its lines and their interrelations.

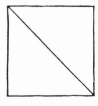

4. LETTER ELEMENTS. Letters, considered as geometrical figures, have these same properties. We speak of the length and directions of the lines of which letters are built. But the names we give to the properties of the whole letters are different. The quantity or area of a letter we speak of as its *weight*. The quality or shape of a letter we call its *character*. The diagrams in the margin are taken from the first book of Euclid's *Elements*. These three figures give the geometric forms of A, C, D, G, I, L, N, and O.

5. CORRECTIONS. The A, N, and O are drawn with the same actual widths. But for a variety of reasons they do not appear so to

the eye. The triangular A looks narrower, and the square N looks wider, than the circular O. The eye craves a certain uniformity in what it reads, and to satisfy it, we reduce the width of N until it appears to be that of O. The other letters are defined geometrically in a similar way, being made of lines with lengths and directions, and constituting plane figures with areas and shapes. These, too, need usually to be corrected as to width. Such geometric figures and their necessary corrections are the formal basis of our letters.

CHAPTER 2. LETTER TECHNIQUES

1. TECHNIQUE. Art is the imposition of ideas on material by certain means for an end. In the art of lettering, the corrected forms are the ideas which are imposed. The means by which they are imposed are the energy of the artist, his hands, and the various tools these hands hold, directing and giving their own character to that energy. As in other arts, the material chosen and the tools by which it is reshaped are so intimately related that they are given a common name—technique. The corrected forms are skeletons. These skeletons are now to be clothed with flesh. This materialization of the mental skeletons will modify them, for the characteristics of the materials and of the tools concerned will set their seal upon the previously immaterial mental forms. The basic techniques by which letters are made are three: marking, writing, and incising.

2. LINES, STROKES, AND CUTS. Lines, straight or curved, are indications of directions, continuous or changing. They have only enough actual width to make them visible, and therefore legible. The technique by which letters are composed of lines is *marking*. Strokes, straight or curved, are lines to which the factor of breadth has been added. They have, therefore, not only the property of direction, but also that of area. The technique by which letters are composed of strokes is *writing*, whether the tool be the pen or the brush. Cuts, straight or curved, are strokes which are sunk below a surface, and therefore have not only directior and area, but also depth. The technique by which letters are composed of cuts is *incising*, whether the tool be the chisel or the gouge.

9

3. DIRECTIONS. The lead pencil and the stylus are common marking tools, and can make very thin lines. The thinner these lines are, the more letters made from them are like mental forms— mere combinations of directions and lengths. Marked letters are thus useful in making a transition between the world of ideas and the world of objects. When, with a pencil or stylus, you have marked corrected skeletons on your ultimate material, the process of materialization has begun. Marked letters thus help in spacing and arrangement.

4. THICKS AND THINS. Writing pens and writing brushes make strokes of a definite width, and it is obvious that this width varies with the direction in which the tool moves, and the angle at which it is held. Thus not only curved letters like O acquire a new character, but also angular letters like N. Only I, a single stroke of unvarying direction, is unaffected by changes in thickness. In writing, the strokes of letters acquire meaning in terms of surface, and therefore area or weight. The quality of thicks and thins which the writing tool gives to letters is called *graphic*.

5. SERIFS. The normal way to make letters permanent on a stone surface is to cut them into it with a chisel. A straight V cut, so incised, is finished up most neatly at its end with a little triangular plane. The cleaning up of this little triangle almost inevitably means the widening of the square end of the whole cut, so that what were originally right angles become more acute. Incising thus naturally results in the widening of the ends of straight members, and such widenings are called *serifs*. Qualities which incising tools give to letters are called *glyptic*.

6. IDEAL AND ACTUAL FORMS. Not only does the mind have its effect upon material things, but what happens among materials reacts again upon the mind. This is difficult to discuss because the word *form* is used both for the mental image of things and for their actual essence when made. The form of a letter A is the idea or image of that letter seen with the inner eye of the imagination. But it is also the pattern in which ink is arranged on a paper surface so as to cause the existence of an actual A, capable of being seen with the outer eye. A purely mental form has

10

no material existence, but is capable of being expressed in matter. When it has been so expressed, the form has been made actual. We call the purely mental image an *ideal form*, and the same image when it informs material, an *actual form*.

7. INTERACTION. Ideal forms, having only a subjective existence, are clothed with matter and become the forms of things with objective existence. This actual existence is expressed in terms of the technique that has been used. The material so formed is seen by the eye, and the form is judged by the mind. If the mind finds any lack in what it thus sees, it creates a new and corrected image, a new ideal form which is again ready to be materialized. Thus there is a perpetual interaction between the world of thoughts and the world of things, between the realm of ideas and that of paper and ink, stone and chisels. The acceptance by the mind of the stone serif, which we have just noticed, is an example.

8. DEVELOPED FORM. But this process of action and reaction between subject and object need not go on forever. The mind soon becomes adjusted to the objective facts, and the technical facts to the mind. When this equilibrium has been reached, the process of development is completed, and remains so until some change in function, technique or imagination disturbs the balance. But until this happens the forms remain more or less unchanging, and are called *developed forms*.

9. TECHNICAL SUMMARY. The development of the letter forms may be summarized thus. The skeletons conceived in geometric terms become marked letters in the world of objects. These letters are then corrected by the mind to suit the mechanics of sight. These corrected forms are then used as paths for writing tools to follow, and the resulting letters thus acquire thicks and thins. These graphic forms return again to the mind, and become the images for incised letters. In the technique of cutting they acquire serifs. This glyptic character is in turn accepted by the mind as a reasonable part of the developed letter. Such letters are mentally established in terms of *knowledge*, acquired by actual technical experience. In our Western tradition, the first set of developed forms for letters are those of Roman inscription capitals.

11

CHAPTER 3. LETTER FUNCTIONS

1. LEGIBILITY. The goodness, or use, of letters is their legibility. It is the function of letters to be read, to be the instruments of conveying ideas from one mind to another. So legible letters are made up of legible strokes legibly arranged.

2. VOIDS AND SOLIDS. Letters are made up of strokes, but the empty spaces between and around them are as important to legibility as the strokes themselves. In written letters the white spaces of paper between the black ink strokes, in incised letters the smooth spaces of surface between the cuts, are as important to the reader as the ink strokes and the chisel cuts themselves. We call the pen strokes and the chisel cuts the *solids* of lettering, and the spaces between them the *voids*.

3. UNITY. Legibility in letters, both of solids and voids, depends to a great extent upon a certain similarity between them. The general purpose of lettering is to convey a message from the mind of the writer to that of the reader, and this purpose is defeated if there is too much diversity between the various strokes and various letters, so that some of them attract undue attention to themselves. Like a well-drilled army, good letters wear a uniform, and act in a uniform way—as an orderly group, not as a rabble of individuals. They work in common, and must accept the discipline of a certain community of appearance.

4. DIVERSITY. But the letters must also be clearly distinguishable from each other or a worse confusion will result. An O must not be taken for a D, nor a B for an E. Unless the ways in which the various letters differ from each other are sufficiently emphasized there is danger of confusion between them. Legibility thus depends upon a nice balance between Unity and Diversity, Likeness and Unlikeness.

PART C. THE PROBLEM OF WORK

CHAPTER 1. SIMPLICITY OF CAUSES

1. INTRODUCTION. It now remains to give certain pieces of practical advice, which enlarge upon what we have said in both preceding parts, and serve to bind them together. Each one of these five rules is really, when reduced to its very core, no more than a way of saying *Know what you have to do. Don't get muddled.* Each suggests practical ways of keeping the mind on the real problem, and of avoiding the confusion and disorder which are so deadly to any kind of good work.

2. SIMPLICITY. By keeping all the artistic essentials—purpose, material, tools and image—as simple as possible, they are more controllable by the mind than if they are complex, and there will be least chance of confusion.

3. PURPOSE. A simple purpose is easier to fulfill than a complicated and involved one. It is better to consider mere legibility as the aim of a piece of writing than legibility plus beauty, plus expression of the writer's personality, plus a high fee, plus the establishment of a reputation as a calligrapher. There are too many cross currents in the complex purpose, and the conflict of these is confusing to the artist. If the primary aim is to be achieved, it is necessary to let the secondary aims take care of themselves.

4. MATERIAL. It is better to carve letters in a piece of simple wood than in a piece of plywood. In the plywood you have successive layers of grain running in opposite directions. The same tool, held at the same angle, will have different effects on the different layers.

5. TOOLS. A few simple tools are better than many, and complicated ones. It takes a long time to learn the potentialities of any one tool, and life is certainly too short to get the best out of many. Complicated tools are more restricted in their use than simple ones, and therefore more of these must be used. With a knife you can do a thousand tasks; with a pencil sharpener you can only sharpen pencils.

6. IMAGE. And obviously, the simpler the images, the more

13

clearly they may be seen in the mind, and the more directly they can be transferred to the material. Many a work of art suffers a loss of its formal quality in the transference of form to matter. The simpler the form, the less the danger of such loss.

7. COMBINATION. And lastly, the simpler all these essentials are, the easier it is to relate them to each other. The perfection of the thing made, which we perceive as its beauty, depends upon a harmonious adjustment between all the artistic factors. This adjustment takes place in the mind. Other things being equal, the simpler the elements combined, the more perfect will be the harmony of their combination.

Chapter 2. ULTIMACY OF CAUSES

1. REALITIES. The artistic causes are the realities of the artistic process. They are what really make the object of art what it is. Therefore the more we can know about these realities, and the less we have to rely on guessing, the truer our ideas will be, and the better we shall be able to guide and direct the whole affair.

2. PURPOSE. If a piece of lettering is to be used, that is, to be read, under certain conditions, it is best that it should be designed and made under those same conditions. The effects of distance, light, color, angle, etc., can then be judged on the spot, and adjustments made while this is still possible. Whenever you can, you should write or carve inscriptions *in situ*.

3. MATERIAL. For the same reason the inscription that is ultimately to be carved in stone should not be designed in watercolor, nor in clay, nor in wood, but should be designed in its ultimate material. Here again, you do not have to guess, you know. The aesthetic check cannot be used unless you work thus with ultimate realities. Your aesthetic conscience tells you that something is wrong at such and such a part of your work. But when you design granite letters in plaster, or wooden letters in clay, so much else is wrong that the warning voice is smothered.

4. TOOLS. And so with instruments. As far as possible letters that are to be written with a brush should be designed with a brush.

14

Stencils of letters that are to be made with a knife should be designed with a knife. The best incised letters are thought out by their designer, chisel in hand. The last tool to be used should be, as far as possible, also the first tool, for the first tool decides the shape and the last tool is the one that really does the job.

5. IMAGE. And so likewise with the imagination. The imagination that sees the image first should if possible be the same that sees it last. The designer should be the craftsman. If the design is conceived by one man, recorded in some way, and then this record is given to another to impose on material, there is a danger of misinterpretation which should be avoided whenever that is possible. A composer cannot play his symphony all by himself, nor a playwright put on a play without other artists to cooperate with him, but a letter designer can carve his own inscriptions, and a letter carver can design them. When the first imagination is also the ultimate imagination, the designer does not have to guess, he knows.

6. REALISM. So the letterer is wise who sticks as closely as possible to the ultimate realities of his problem. When he can, he works *in situ*, in the ultimate material, with the ultimate tools, and he himself thinks out his design with the same mind with which he will impose it. So doing, he is able to deal with his problem more realistically than in any other way.

CHAPTER 3. CONSCIOUSNESS OF CAUSES

1. INTIMACY. We have noticed that the factors with which the artist deals are some more and some less intimately connected with himself. The ideally perfect artist is he whose work, by a lifetime of practice, has become part of himself, who can design with no conscious effort, who has succeeded, as the Orientals say, in *becoming his own Work*.

2. PURPOSE. But artists are not ideally perfect. When you are a beginner, many of the realities of your art are strange to you. Furthest away from yourself and your interests is the purpose of the thing to be made. This is really more your patron's business

15

than it is yours, but you must make it sufficiently your own to be able to produce an object that will serve that purpose, or you are no artist. To do this you must keep it constantly in mind, and this concentration is not achieved without an effort. To serve purpose as it should be served requires at first much self-conscious discipline.

3. MATERIAL. The right use of material comes more easily to the designer. If you practice long enough with any material, your mind at last comes to work in terms of it. Michael Angelo boasted that he had marble dust in his blood—that marble had entered into his soul. When the letter cutter thinks of letters in terms of marble and limestone, or the calligrapher in terms of paper and ink, the material has become part of his mind, and he can forget about it. He will no more abuse it than he will hold his own finger in the flame of a candle.

4. TOOLS. And similarly, the tool can become by constant practice an even more integral part of the designer than material itself. It is an extension of his hand. As a blind man feels with the end of his stick, as if the stick had nerve endings at its tip, so the penman feels with the end of his quill or reed, and the cutter with the end of his chisel. The tool becomes part of the designer's body, and the characters it gives to the design,—thicks and thins, serifs,—become part of his mind. When they have fully done so, he can forget about them.

5. THE HAND. Considered as a tool, the hand itself is merely a slightly more intimate part of the designer than his pen or chisel. When the hand also becomes trained, it too can be forgotten. What we call the training of the hand is really the development in the mind of manual kinaesthetic images.

6. IMAGE. And when we reach the imagination we have reached the center of the artist himself. The imagination need not become part of the artist. It is, by nature, already a part of him. It can be trained in various ways, but in its moment of activity it must be free,—let alone by the conscious part of the mind,—or it simply won't work. Like the material and the tool we must learn how to handle it, and then learn to forget its existence.

16

7. ERRORS. If you do not understand these principles, there is a grave danger that you will fall into artistic errors which are common. Such are abuse of the material, technical showing off, instrumental and manual virtuosity, and lastly, imaginative paralysis, and that falling back on derivatism which inevitably follows it.

CHAPTER 4. ORDER OF CAUSES

1. DIFFICULTY. It is easy to say: Follow out the purpose; let the material express itself; allow the tool to follow its bent; do not force the imagination,—but just how are these commands to be carried out? It is obvious that if the material were allowed to do exactly what it wants to do, it would have to be let alone, for all art implies a certain violence against the nature of material. How is a proper balance between control and liberty to be achieved? The following order of procedure, and the exercises recommended, may help to answer these questions.

2. PURPOSE AND TECHNIQUE. Before we make anything we must know what we are going to make—a chair, a book, a house, a cup. The starting point in any making is the purpose of the thing to be made. When we have the purpose clear, say the representation of a fish, to be legible at a certain distance, our second task is to decide on the technique best suited to the realization of that purpose. Let us say that we decide to use paper and ink and to handle them with a pointed water-color brush.

3. TECHNICAL SHAPES. The third step is to find out what are the specific shapes that these materials and this tool most naturally produce. This may take much practice. The best Chinese painters have spent their lives on it. But it is a stage that cannot be neglected. We must know at least something of what the ink-laden brush *wants to do*. Beautiful things are made up of beautiful parts, and the parts will not be beautiful unless their shapes are the best the technique can supply.

4. SHAPES APPLIED. Fourth, having learned something about brush strokes, we study the problem of the representation in terms of them. How can these strokes best be combined to state the neces-

sary truths about a fish? Notice that there is no attempt here to sketch the appearance of the object to be represented, but to express its essence.

5. KINAESTHESIS. The fifth is the translation of this visual image into a kinaesthetic one. This means the rapid writing of the sign over and over again, until it becomes established as a muscular pattern. Our hand now knows what to do without any dictation from the eye. The pattern has acquired a looseness and freedom, a quality of *drawing*, which it did not have at first.

6. ADJUSTMENT. But the likeness to a fish has been sadly damaged. The sixth step is to adjust the kinaesthetic pattern to suit the eye. This adjustment should keep as much as possible of the kinaesthetic freedom just gained, but discipline it by reference to visual order.

7. FINAL CHECK. And lastly, check this adjusted pattern, now suited both to hand and eye, to see if it is a sufficient solution of the original problem of representation. If it fulfills the purpose, your task is at an end.

8. PRACTICE. Exercises of this sort are most valuable for the designer of letters. Draw simple pictures in this way, a fish, a cat, a fly, a knot, the ocean, an eye. You will be surprised to find how difficult these problems are, and how they bring out the principles of design. Try them all again with other techniques, with a broad-nibbed pen, with the finger in the sand, by bending short pieces of soft wire. Such exercises as these, extended over thousands of years, lie behind the letters we use today. If you spend time on them you will find that you know more about the inner nature of letters, and of many other arts, than ever you did before.

Chapter 5. STAGES

1. BUILDING. The exercise just described is divided into seven steps, or stages, and the process of making anything that may be made divides up naturally into stages in a similar way. A novel, or a house, must go through an orderly series of processes if its building is to be successful.

18

2. CLARITY. One rule in the handling of stages is that each should be seen clearly in the mind in advance. Not only has the ultimate stage its image, but each milestone along the way has an equally clear form. To borrow an analogy from nature, notice the stages in the development of a butterfly. There are separate patterns for the egg, for the larva, for the pupa, and for the imago. Each is distinct from the others, and of a separate character.

3. PERFECTION. Another rule is that you should complete each stage as perfectly as possible, in all its parts, before going on to the next. It is well to do this even when certain parts of your work in an early stage will be destroyed by a later one. It is better to take time to keep your mind clear, than to try to save it at the expense of confusion and muddle.

4. CAUSES. Stages are in most cases defined by the particular technique that is characteristic of that part of the work. Sometimes the material changes, sometimes the tool, sometimes both. Sometimes the stage is determined chiefly by formal considerations. But to the extent that each stage has its own causes, it is worthy of the artist's best effort. The ultimate stage is not the only one he should strive to perfect, even if it is the only one that anyone else will ever see.

5. SUPERMEN. The reward of working methodically by stages is clarity and serenity of mind. You need not superhuman intelligence and courage to tackle a complex problem if you take it in an orderly way. For most of us, the tackling of a problem needing superhuman intelligence and courage, is one which we merely bungle, for we are not supermen. Working by orderly stages enables mere men to perform apparently superhuman tasks.

Chapter 6. CONCLUSION

1. TRUTH AND ACTION. The end of theoretical knowledge is Truth, while that of practical knowledge is Action. We cannot act until we know. This first book is theoretical; its purpose is to clear up our minds about the business of making letters, so that we may go on to the practical book without mental confusion and

19

false notions. With a certain amount of Truth to guide us, we can take up, with some hope of success, the practical business of making letters.

2. TRUTH. Truth is a relation of congruity between what is outside our minds and what is inside them. If I think a certain sheet of a white substance is vellum, and the fact agrees with my thought, you can say my thought is true. Or you can say that what I hold is real and true vellum. Falsehood is the lack of this agreement between thoughts and things.

3. TRUE LETTERS. There is much imperfect lettering in the world today, and this is chiefly because false ideas about lettering are so generally accepted. What people think about letters, and the actual facts, do not agree. And we cannot act properly unless we think properly. This whole first book is an attempt to state certain fundamental truths, so that true letters—letters that are actually what they seem to be—may be made. These will always be found also to be good letters,—legible; and beautiful letters, —admirable.

4. FIVE RULES. By keeping the causes of letters simple, by keeping these causes real, by understanding their degrees of identity with ourselves, by handling them in proper relation to each other, and by the understanding of stages, we can keep our minds so clear about the facts of lettering that we shall have no excuse for becoming confused. If we follow these principles, we should have little difficulty in avoiding the pitfalls that beset letter designers today.

5. DERIVATISM. Contemporary letter design too often consists in making new copies of old letters, regardless of their causes. The origin of the new letter so made is not a mental form, but a material shape. The copyist is not free, because he is tied to the effects of past conditions having little to do with his own problem. He cannot often produce good and useful letters, because his derivatism forces him to repeat shapes that are fully legible only under conditions which no longer exist. He does not produce true letters, because what his letters are and what they seem to be are not the same. And only by accident can he produce beautiful letters, because the beauty of any material thing is a radiance of its

20

own perfection, and cannot, without loss, be transferred to it from perfect things with other natures.

6. FREEDOM. The letterer must know what his problems truly are before he can be free to work out real solutions to them. It is truth that makes him free. Unless he is an original artist, he cannot count on producing letters that are beautiful, true or good—admirable, genuine or legible.

BOOK TWO

THE PRACTICAL ELEMENTS

PART A. IMAGE
Letters as Things to be Imagined

PART B. TECHNIQUE
Letters as Things to be Made

PART C. FUNCTION
Letters as Things to be Read

THE PRACTICAL ELEMENTS
PART A. IMAGE
CHAPTER 1. INTRODUCTION

1. NATURALISM. Because they are unable to create new images suited to the requirements of the new thing to be made, designers of feeble imagination generally fall back on imitating the effects of natural and artificial things. But for the letterer there is little temptation to be naturalistic. We know fantastic alphabets that have imitated the appearance of tree-trunks or foliage, but in general letters have no relation to things produced by nature, and there is little tendency to copy them.

2. DERIVATISM. There is, however, a strong tendency to copy the work of other men. Roman capitals have been made for two thousand years, and most of the other forms descended from these for nearly as long. Innumerable masters have written and cut letters, and traditional solutions have become established. It is as easy as it is common to copy such shapes; but such derivative copying is the chief enemy of good lettering today—the unintelligent copying of visual shapes, which do not fit the problem to be solved, rather than the intelligent development of original forms, which do fit. Unless you understand this, a superficial knowledge of techniques will be little help to good design.

3. INSIGHT. You will never see good letters coming from your hand until you have learned to see good letters in your head. Good work depends on clear mental images. Clear images are based on knowledge of the causes of the things imagined. Knowledge comes from intelligent practice. When practice has given the artist a clear image of what he has to do, he has insight into his art.

CHAPTER 2. SKELETONS

1. ABSTRACTION. To understand letters truly we must begin by ignoring all the qualities they have acquired from being put to particular uses, all the qualities with which particular techniques have endowed them, and all the fanciful variants with which the

25

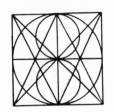

ABCDEFGHKL
MNOPQRST
XYZ
IJUVW
AOZ
LDE
B

I. LINEAR FIGURES

26

II. PLANE FIGURES

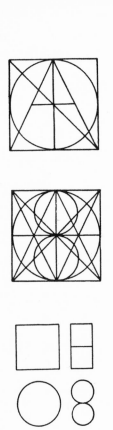

imaginations of particular peoples and individuals have enriched them. We must start with letters reduced to their very simplest terms.

2. LINES AND PLANES. We think of letters as configurations of lines, with lengths and directions; and we also think of them as configurations of surfaces, or as shaped areas. These are two different ways of thinking about the same letters, but we shall see the essential nature of the problem more easily if we think of these aspects separately, and only later on unite them. Plates I and II show the simplest possible versions of our alphabet, expressed first as linear and then as plane figures. How are the figures arrived at?

3. LINEAR FIGURES. If we superimpose the three Euclidean figures shown earlier, we get the upper diagram. It contains twelve out of the twenty-six letters of our alphabet. By adding other lines we get the second diagram, containing all our letters except W, which is really not a single letter, but two V's set together. Plate I gives all the letters separated from the diagram, and arranged with an equal horizontal distance between them of $\frac{1}{4}$ of the letter height. Where the diagram offers us a choice of forms, as the half-width or the full-width, E or H, we are guided by the principle of one- and two-storey figures. The first class are those based on single large squares, circles and semicircles; the second on two smaller squares, circles, or semicircles, one upon the other. Thus the one-storey H is full-, and the two-storey E, half-width. The curves are all true arcs of circles. The straight lines and curves, as in the diagrams, are drawn with mechanical instruments.

4. PLANE FIGURES. To express these figures in terms of surface, Plate II, we follow the simplest procedure we can. Some of them, as O, D, and B, already completely enclose their characteristic surfaces. Others, as N, can do so only if we regard the ruled horizontals as part of their figures. In still others, as Z, it is necessary to add verticals in order to enclose an area. And, finally, there are some forms, like L, which need the addition of a diagonal between their salient points. I, alone, by its nature as a line with only one direction, cannot be expressed in terms of surface.

28

THE IMAGES OF LETTERS

5. LINEAR UNIFORMITY AND DIVERSITY. The primary function of letters is to be legible. The figures in Plate I are not true letters, but are expressions of the linear aspect of letters. They are useful to us, if they help us to understand the part which lines play in legibility. As legibility depends upon a just balance between uniformity and diversity, the linear arrangements must be like enough to be able to work together without calling attention to any particular figure, and unlike enough to be easily distinguishable.

6. LINEAR LEGIBILITY. These figures are satisfactory in their differences. Although composed of similar elements, these are arranged in such diverse and characteristic ways that there is no danger of the figures being confused with one another. And these figures are legible for another reason. Because we arrange letters between horizontal lines, all of them have the same height, and have the legibility that comes from the fact that no one, by reason of tallness or shortness, calls undue attention to itself.

7. LINEAR ILLEGIBILITY. But from the point of view of widths, these figures are too diverse. Taking the letter height as the unit, we find five different widths. Such letters as A, O, and Z are of full-width; L, D, and E are half-width, B is quarter-width. I has the minimum width of a mere line, and W has the special width of two letter heights. These five widths are too many for necessary uniformity. I is exceptional, but something can be done with the other classes shown.

8. FIGURE UNIFORMITY AND DIVERSITY. The areas in Plate II are not themselves true letters, but are the statement of aspects of true letters which will be useful if they help us to understand this problem of legibility. These surface arrangements must be like enough to each other to do their work harmoniously, but unlike enough so that there is no risk of our confusing them.

9. SHAPES OF PLANE FIGURES. The twenty-five plane figures are circles, semicircles, rectangles and triangles, and combinations of these. In the diagram we see the triangle, the circle and the square as the primary figures; the half triangle, the semicircle and the half square as the secondary figures; and the double semicircle as the tertiary figure. Their necessary uniformity would be

29

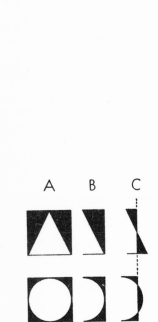

A B C

BOOK TWO: PRACTICAL ELEMENTS

increased if the shapes of these seven figures could in some way be unified.

10. AREAS OF PLANE FIGURES. Here we consider the plane figures as quantities. Again taking the letter height as one linear unit, we get one square unit for the area of the square. The area of the circle is, however, only .7854 of a square unit. For our purposes we may consider this fraction as $\frac{3}{4}$, the error of $3\frac{1}{2}$ per cent being negligible. The area of the triangle is $\frac{1}{2}$ a square unit. Similarly the half triangle is $\frac{1}{4}$, the semicircle $\frac{3}{8}$, and the half square $\frac{1}{2}$ a square unit. B has an approximate area value of $^3/_{16}$ a square unit. Without including I and W, we thus have seven classes, ranging from 1 to $^3/_{16}$ a square unit in area. These seven differ too much in area for uniformity.

11. SPACES BETWEEN FIGURES. If we look at Plates I and II we see in a general way what we have been trying to reduce to more exact terms. In Plate I we see that the narrowest letters are too narrow and the widest too wide. In Plate II we see the same thing in terms of weight. There are light, weak spots, and heavy black spots. If we were to print a page of text with the linear figures for letters, and another with the plane figures for letters, we would be even more vividly conscious of the lack of proper uniformity. And when we look at Plates I and II we notice something else. We notice that certain groups of figures seem crowded together, and others openly spaced. G H K in both plates has a close, and U V W an open look. Before we begin to correct the figures we should understand something about the areas and shapes of the spaces *between* them. As the actual number of shapes that may occur between our twenty-six letters is enormous, we reduce the problem to its simplest terms, and examine merely the possible spaces between combinations of the triangle, the circle, and the square.

12. SPACE AREAS. If we place the basic letter figures within squares (A) we find that the triangle leaves an area of $\frac{1}{2}$ a square unit, and the circle $\frac{1}{4}$ a square unit, but the square has no space left outside itself. In interletter spaces we are concerned with the area left on one side of each letter figure, which is for the triangle $\frac{1}{4}$ a square unit, for the circle $\frac{1}{8}$ a square unit, and for the square no

30

area (B). These areas belong partly to the letter figure and partly to the space, so we can divide them by a vertical line in such a way that the space taken within the letter figure equals the space outside of it (C), and this line gives a limit useful in measuring interletter space. The spaces possible between the three figures are shown at D, where they are all placed touching a vertical line, that is, with no linear distance between them. The space areas thus shown vary from $\frac{1}{2}$ a square unit between the triangles to no area between the squares—obviously too great a diversity of area. As the $\frac{1}{2}$ square unit between two triangles cannot be reduced, it serves us as a minimum standard for interletter space. A rectangular interletter space of $\frac{1}{2}$ square unit would have vertical sides $\frac{1}{2}$ linear unit apart. If we draw such verticals and place our letter figures upon them (E) by using the limits arrived at earlier (C), we find equal space areas of $\frac{1}{2}$ square unit between each pair of figures in the second column. In practice, of course, the letterer does not go through all the operations described, but the principles are implicit in the kind of judgments which the mind, guided by the eye, makes. The eye is always the final judge.

13. APPARENT WIDTH. The vertical line which defines the limit between one side of a letter figure and its space, may be drawn on each side of the figure. So drawn, these verticals define a rectangle equal in area to the figure. The width of this rectangle gives the apparent width of the figure. Spaces are kept equal in area by keeping the distances between the apparent widths of adjacent letters equal.

14. CORRECTIONS. Among the linear figures some are too narrow and some too wide. Among the plane figures some are too weak and some too strong. The semicircular figures were particularly noticeable among the narrow and weak, and the square figures among the wide and strong. Apparent width is the unifying principle by which these extremes may be modified. The area of the circle is a mean between that of the triangle and that of the square. Therefore we take the area of the circle as the norm for the wider letters, and reduce the square figures to rectangles having that area. We are changing the extreme areas only, and as the triangle

31

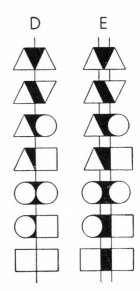

is not one of these, it remains without change. But the weak semi-circle is strengthened by increasing its area to that of the circle. The figures containing small semicircles are proportionately increased. This reduces the three classes to two, the wide and the narrow, D taking its place as a wide letter with A, O, and Z, and B taking its place with L and E. The apparent widths of the corrected figures are now $\frac{1}{2}$ for A, $\frac{3}{4}$ for O, $\frac{3}{4}$ for Z, $\frac{3}{4}$ for D, $\frac{1}{4}$ for L, $\frac{1}{2}$ for E, and $\frac{3}{8}$ for B, all between $\frac{1}{4}$ and $\frac{3}{4}$. These fractions also give the areas for the figures. For various reasons which can be understood by study, T, X, Y, and Z are also best reduced to the apparent width of the circle.

15. APPARENT HEIGHT. As we read horizontally from left to right, our corrections are chiefly concerned with widths, and we are not seriously disturbed by varieties in apparent height, although these are a slight interference with uniformity. The letters are actually of the same height, but because they reach the horizontal parallels in different ways, they do not all appear to be so. The square meets the ruled parallels with flat faces, either actually drawn as in Z, or implied as in H, but because the triangle meets them at an angular point, and the circle at a point of tangency, both of these apparently just miss their objective. We therefore make triangular figures a little higher, and circular figures a little larger, than the actual distance between the ruled lines. In the same way we draw the interior acute angles of M and N just outside the writing line. In practice also we often make Z or T a little less than one unit in height, to prevent them from seeming too high.

16. STASIS. This concludes our discussion of corrections for legibility. Legibility is the basic function of lettering, and it is achieved by means of the eye. But besides the sense of sight there are two others which may be satisfied or dissatisfied with letters, though their claims are secondary. Stasis and Kinaesthesis are concerned, and the demands of these senses have a certain part in the correction of the figures. The static sense enables us to keep our balance. Sympathy means feeling with the feelings of other people, and by sympathy we like to see other people, and even inanimate things, stable, just as we like to be stable ourselves. We feel in this

32

way even about letters, and although they are not really things that can tip over, we tend to think of them as if they could, and are happier when they can be made in a way which looks as if they balanced.

17. MIDDLE DIVISION. This static sympathy is probably largely responsible for certain corrections in letters which have a top and a bottom half, though there are doubtless other psychological factors involved. In such letters as B there is a tendency to raise the middle division slightly, so as to lower the apparent center of gravity. In other letters, as A, the middle division is lowered, as this gives a greater appearance of stability.

18. KINAESTHESIS. The kinaesthetic sense informs us of the activities of our own muscles. Letters are seen with the eye, but they are made with the hand, and manual convenience is as important to the maker of letters, as visual convenience is important to the reader. Letters, therefore, may be thought of as patterns of muscular movements. The line that the hand makes most easily is the flat curve. When the semicircle of C or D is increased to the apparent width of O, the extra width may be given either by continuing the curves, or flattening them out into horizontal lines. The kinaesthetic action of the hand compromises between the true arc and the straight line, by the use of a flat curve. The flattened middle portion of the S is also kinaesthetic, making an easier transition for the hand in its change of direction.

19. CORRECTED SKELETONS. Plate III shows the figures of Plate I corrected visually for the benefit of the reading eye, statically to satisfy the desire for stability, and kinaesthetically for the convenience of the writing hand. We call these corrected figures *Skeletons*. They are the bones of the capital alphabet, bones as yet unclothed with flesh. They are the paths along which the tool which is to materialize them will actually travel. Like the lines of the figures on Plate I, they are statements of direction and length, but they are statements not merely of geometric concepts, but of these, corrected to suit the senses.

20. STUDY. This skeleton alphabet is only one solution to the problem of correcting letters in their simplest form to meet the

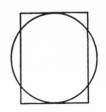

33

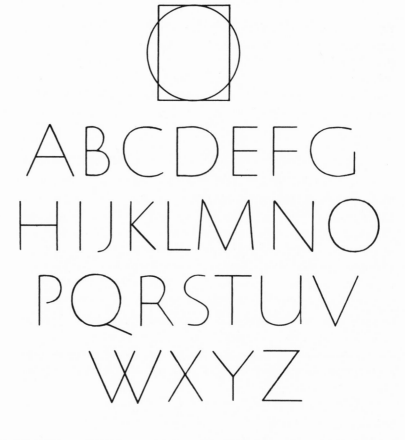

ABCDEFG
HIJKLMNO
PQRSTUV
WXYZ

ℒℰℊℎℳℳℴℳℳℴℳℳℳ

ᗝℯℊℎℳℳℴ

III. CORRECTED SKELETONS

34

practical needs of maker and user. Other calligraphers produce alphabets somewhat different, but just as satisfactory. This solution, however, is that of the authors of this treatise, and the reader will not get the best out of it unless he studies these skeletons well, and commits their structure to memory, for they will serve him as the basis for future technical experiment.

Chapter 3. OTHER SKELETONS

1. DEVELOPMENTS. Today we use other alphabets beside those of which the corrected skeletons are the essential forms. These letters developed from the capitals by a variety of causes, chiefly kinaesthetic and technical. They may be expressed as skeletons, and since these will serve as paths for writing tools to follow, you must study their structure carefully, until they are familiar to your hand as well as your eye.

2. ROUND FORMS. We show variants that differ from the capitals by the substitution of curved lines for angular combinations in many letters. These are not in common use today, and should therefore be used sparingly, though suited to certain decorative purposes. These skeletons form a transition between the capitals and the small letters.

3. SMALL LETTERS. Plate IV gives the skeletons of the small Roman letters, in which the capital forms have been still further modified by roundness, and also by the extension of verticals. Some of the skeletons are the same, as O, S, and V; others, as A, B, and D, are quite different from the capitals. But the most important distinction is that capitals are contained in one space between two lines, and small letters in three equal spaces between four. The special diagram is constructed by drawing a circle with a diameter of half the capital letter height, drawing verticals limiting the apparent width of the circle, and extending these verticals to the top and bottom horizontal lines. The variants for a, g, i, l, and t, at the bottom of the plate, are forms suited to certain special uses.

4. ITALICS. Plate V gives the skeletons of the Italic letters, with a few variant forms. The special diagram is constructed

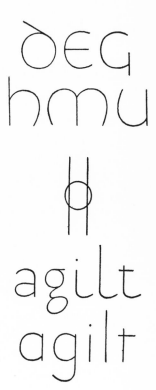

35

abcdefghij

klmnopqr

stuvwxyz

agilt

IV. SMALL SKELETONS

36

abcdefgh
ijklmnopqrs
tuvwxyz
agkwy

V. ITALIC SKELETONS

37

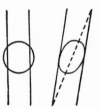

thus. Draw parallel lines the same horizontal distance apart as are the verticals in the preceding diagram, but *tilted* to the right not more than 10° from the vertical. A diagonal from the bottom of the first to the top of the second parallel gives the angle of *slope* measured from the vertical, and becomes the axis of the loop of the letter, an oval contained between parallels. The a and g have the simpler of the alternative shapes for these letters. Study particularly the relationships, in this alphabet, between the straight and the curved elements. This is an important factor in all linear design, and is fundamental in the construction of italics. The main characteristics of this alphabet are compression, uniformity of width, and uniformity of tilts and slopes. These are among the *cursive* qualities which freely written alphabets tend to show, so called from their running or flowing character.

5. NUMERALS. Arabic numerals are not descended from Roman skeletons, but the tools by which they are made follow paths, and these paths may be marked as lines. They have two versions. *Ranging* numerals are for use with capitals, and like them are contained between two horizontal lines. *Non-ranging* numerals are for use with small letters, and are written in three spaces between four horizontals. The English usage in non-ranging numerals is to drop the odd numbers to touch the bottom horizontal and raise the even numbers to touch the top one. But this is not the convention in this country, where the ascending and descending numerals are usually arranged as we show them.

6. AMPERSAND. The symbol that stands for the English word *and* is often put at the end of the alphabet as if it were a sort of twenty-seventh letter. It is a monogram for E and T, the letters of *and* in Latin. It is the only monogram that has been sufficiently used to have earned a place among the letters, where it really has as much right as the monogram we call W.

38

PART B. TECHNIQUE

SECTION I. Marking

1. TOOLS. We divide the tools of lettering into those used for marking, for writing, and for incising. Here we discuss marking tools, which produce lines, whether straight or curved, whose lengths and directions are of importance, but whose widths are negligible. The tools most used for making such lines today are the graphite pencil, hard or soft, the ruling pen, the stylus, and the steel-pointed *crowquill* pen. Except for the last these may be used with rulers for the making of straight, and with compasses for the making of curved, lines.

2. FUNCTION. If the imagination were capable of holding images indefinitely complicated, the letterer would have little use for marking, but the imagination being what it is, this technique is valuable as the means by which a certain early stage in design is recorded. Marked lines are useful as forming a link between creative plans in the world of thoughts, and actual material letters in the world of things. The stronger the designer's imagination, and the more clearly he can see a complicated arrangement of letters in his mind's eye, the less need he will have for recording the early stages of the design by means of marking.

3. COMPOSITION SKETCH. When the letterer has been given his text, his first task is to arrange it broadly in relation to the thing it is to be written or carved on. This is done in a small composition sketch made freely with soft pencil. The letters are indicated to no particular scale, and with soft pencil, in order that there may be the maximum of kinaesthetic freedom. Graphite is slippery, a true lubricant, and the softer it is the more easily it glides over the paper, and the less resistance the tool sets up to the free expression of images. The hard pencil is for drawings whose purpose is to define measures and positions accurately, but it is an impediment to the designer who tries to sketch freely and loosely. To correct its tendency to bite into the paper, the muscles of the hand and arm become tense, and the lines produced correspondingly tight. As large linear letters are extremely deceptive guides to the

THE
ELEMENTS
OF LETTERING

39

spacing of letters which are to be made of strokes, keep your composition sketch small, so that the actual thickness of the pencil line approximates the weight of the strokes when the sketch is translated into full size.

4. SCALE SKETCH. When the arrangement of the main mass of the lettering and the heights of the various lines are thus roughly determined, the scheme is transferred to an accurate scale drawing of the surface to be lettered. The lines and margins are accurately ruled with a hard pencil, and the letters again freely indicated by marking between the rulings with a soft one.

5. FULL–SIZE LAYOUT. The same principles govern the making of the full-size drawing. The guide lines are accurately marked, and the letters are freely written within them with a pen or brush. Unless the ruling is exact and accurate, the final result is injured by a disorderly beginning. Freedom in detail is only possible when there has been due thought for order in the general plan.

6. LINEAR LETTERS. Under exceptional conditions it is sometimes reasonable to make linear letters not to act as paths for a writing tool to follow, but to exist in their own right. If you have occasion to make such letters, attention to two points will help you to avoid trouble. First, as the letters are made of lines of minimum thickness, use some true marking technique, such as mechanical drawing with ruling pen or pencil. And secondly, keep the shapes close to the corrected skeletons, for they are essentially linear and the best forms for linear letters. Engraving on metal, or cutting lines on ivory in the manner called *scrimshaw*, are examples of the marking technique.

SECTION II. Writing

CHAPTER 1. MATERIALS AND TOOLS

1. PAPER. The typical writing materials are paper and ink. For ordinary uses almost any good machine-made paper with an unglazed surface makes good writing material. If paper is too smooth —has not enough *tooth*—the pen glides so smoothly over it that the hand has hardly any tactile check on what it is doing. If the surface is too rough, of course the freedom of the pen stroke is in danger. If it is too porous, the ink tends to *feather*. For work that is intended to be as lasting as possible, it is usually better to use a good handmade paper, for in most cases the materials of handmade paper are superior to machine-made. For the finest writing well prepared vellum is the best of all materials, but it should not be used except by the expert calligrapher, whose mind and hand are trained and sure.

2. INK. Black ink is of two general kinds, iron ink, which is essentially a stain, and carbon ink, which is essentially a paint. Iron ink is thin and flows well, but is difficult to get today sufficiently black or permanent. Badly shaped letters written in pale ink look better than they really are, and as learning consists in making mistakes and recognizing them when made, the flattery of inks not really black is a hindrance to the student. The carbon inks are black but are often thick and gummy. A good ink for calligraphic purposes available today is Higgins *Engrossing*. It combines fluidity with blackness. For drawing letters which are to be reproduced by photo-engraving, use a waterproof ink such as Higgins *India*. This, though less fluid, is even blacker than Higgins *Engrossing*, and being waterproof, may be touched up with white to correct errors, a process legitimate only when working for reproduction. Do not use show card white, but special preparations such as *Permo White*, or Schmincke's *Aero White A*.

3. TOOLS. Writing tools are of two general kinds, pens and brushes. Most pens in use today are made of metal by quantity production, but for calligraphy the older materials, feathers from the wings of birds, and the stems of certain plants, cut to the proper shape by their users, are much better. Quills and reeds are the best

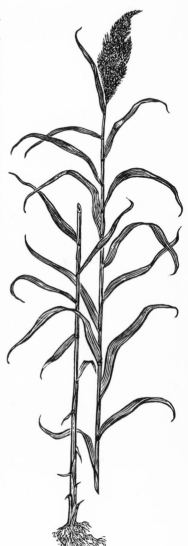

PHRAGMITES
COMMUNIS

41

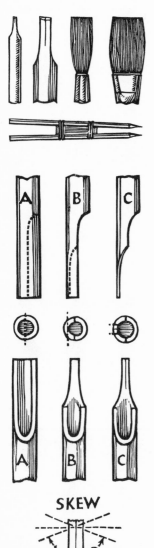

SKEW

tools for the writing of small and medium sized letters. Writing brushes have either round or flat ferrules, and therefore round or flat bunches of hair, both having square, not pointed, tips. They are good for the writing of larger letters, but because less rigid than pens they require far greater dexterity to handle, and are difficult for beginners. The largest letters of all can be laid out with a third kind of tool, the double pencil,—two pencils bound together with string or elastic bands on the opposite sides of a wooden block. The single pencil is a marker, but two pencils thus arranged act as a writing tool—the largest of all. Accordingly we get this series of tools: goose and swan quills, small reeds, large reeds, round and flat ferrule brushes up to the widest that will give an even flow of color, and lastly, the double pencil.

4. REEDS. You can make good reed pens from small shoots of bamboo such as florists and nurserymen use to support potted plants, but much better are the stems of certain large native grasses. As far as we know the best of these is Phragmites Communis, which grows in swampy ground throughout the northeastern parts of the United States. The Sea Oat, Uniola Panniculata, growing in sandy soil near the sea, from Virginia to Texas, is another good writing reed, better than bamboo, but we have had less experience with it. There are doubtless other plants, in other parts of the country, which could be used for the making of good pens. If you use bamboo, choose a large piece, three-eighths of an inch in diameter, but not less than a quarter of an inch. Select a piece with as large a center hollow, and therefore as thin and compact a wall, as possible. If you use Phragmites, gather only the largest stems, and the part of these nearest the ground, as the wall is apt to be too thin higher up. It should be so strong that you cannot crush the stem in your fingers. If you cannot find Phragmites growing in your neighborhood, consult a botanist at the nearest school or college on the availability of suitable native grasses.

5. CUTTING. You will need a pen-knife and a small block of celluloid or type-metal against which to use it. The small blade of any pocketknife of moderately good steel, with a handle large enough to fit the hand, is good. Keep it sharp and do not use it for

42

other work. Choose a length of reed, and cut it off between joints by rotating the reed against the knife blade held at right angles to it. In the end furthest from a joint make the first cut as shown in A, and the second, B. Do not try to make these cuts with single strokes of the knife, but in a series of parings until you reach the correct shape. Split the end by gently pressing the edge of the knife against it, but do not let the split run back more than one-half an inch. Bracing your thumbs against each other will help you to control this work. Then pare the two sides of the point itself, so as to remove the sharp edges, and trim them so that they are equal on each side of the split. C shows the reed after splitting and trimming. Finally cut off the end against the block. The angle between this cut and the long axis of the shaft is called the *skew*. For various purposes it differs as shown, but for the present make the skew square. When the pen lies horizontally the angle this same cut makes with the horizontal is called the *bevel*. The harder the material of the pen, the sharper the bevel can be, and the sharper the bevel the cleaner the thin strokes it makes. The bevels shown give the limits of those in actual use.

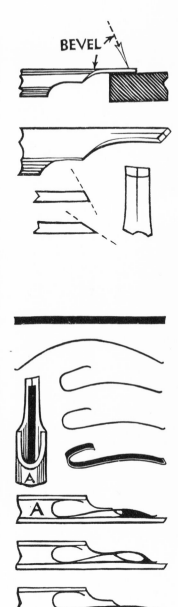

6. SPRINGS. To obviate continual refilling there must be some device for holding a quantity of ink in the pen. Watch repairers usually have a variety of old watch springs on hand, and from one of these you can easily make such a device. Choose a spring a little narrower than the width of the nib you intend to use it with, and break off a piece about twice the length of the cut part of the pen. Be sure to break it *against* and not *with* its natural curvature, as otherwise it may later get stuck in the barrel of the pen. Anneal one-half of the piece by holding it high in the flame of an alcohol lamp, or a match, until the part becomes red hot. Bend back the loop of the annealed end against a small reed, or other rod, and finally adjust to the double curve shown. If the front part arches too high the ink flows too freely; if too low, capillary action draws it back into the barrel. Similarly, if the spring is too far forward there will be too much ink; if too far back, too little. The correct arch and the correct position are shown at A. All reeds and quills used for formal writing need springs.

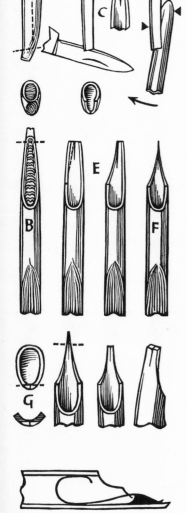

7. QUILLS. The wing feathers of geese make good small quills. If there is a zoo in your neighborhood you can probably get swan and peacock, as well as goose quills, there, especially at the time of the spring and autumn moults. Turkey quills tend to bend when drying, so cut the nib short with a final split of less than $\frac{1}{8}$ of an inch, as the points may otherwise separate after it has been wet with ink. Avoid turkey quills if you can. The stages in cutting a quill are somewhat different from those in cutting a reed. Cut off the tip of the feather, leaving about 9 inches, and strip the barbs from the shaft. Make the cut shown at A and B, being sure that it is exactly in line with the depressed groove on the back of the shaft. Clean out the quill and cut the end straight off, leaving a wide tip, it being difficult to split a quill if the tip is narrow. Next begin the split by pressing the edge of the knife very gently against the end (C), bracing your hands together so as not to let it enter the quill much more than $\frac{1}{16}$ of an inch; lengthen the split by lifting with another quill, or the handle of a small water-color brush, under the nib (D); hold your thumb-nail firmly down on the back of the quill to prevent the split from running too far back. Next pare one side to a complete point (E); and then pare the other side to match it (F). As the inside surface of the quill is concave, pare the under surface of the tip flat (G), or it will make a double line. If the quill has a scaly skin on the back, scrape this off. Cut off the tip so as to give the proper skew and bevel, as with the reed. This last cut should remove all of the first split (C), leaving only the lengthening of it (D).

8. METAL PENS. In spite of the fact that almost all writing is done today with metal nibs, for calligraphy these are inferior to reeds and quills. The advantages of making one's own pen are manifest when one understands how many ways of holding and using a pen are necessary to make various kinds of letters. But there are times when the making of vegetable or animal pens is impossible, and at such times metal ones are a convenience, and satisfactory enough when suited to the particular kind of letters to be made. We show three kinds of metal nibs in common use today. The first is in principle like a reed, cut to make a wide thick

44

and a hair thin stroke. The second gives a wide thick, but a thin about half that width. The third gives a stroke of equal breadth in all directions. Metal pens to suit left-handed writers are rare.

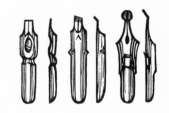

9. DESK. A flat board, so arranged that it may be inclined and held at any angle between 30° and 60° from the horizontal, is the essential part of a desk. By hinging a draughting board to the edge of a table, and arranging an arm, fitted to notches cut in the back, you will have an adequate one. You can make a more portable version of the same thing by hinging two boards together. The angle of the writing surface from the horizontal we call the angle of *inclination*. If too low, the ink flows too freely for good work. Between your paper and the bare board keep a sheet or two of blotting paper. Experiment will tell you how thick and soft this writing pad should be. Across the upper part of the writing paper stretch a tape or large rubber band to keep it in place. Over the lower part fix a strong piece of paper with thumb tacks, to protect the surface not yet written on from contact with your hands.

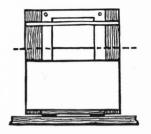

10. ACCESSORIES. You will also need these other tools: to hold the paper flat against the writing pad, a spatula such as the wooden stick doctors use for examining throats; a filler cut from a reed as shown, with which to fill your pen—this should only be long enough to be easy to lift out of the bottle, for otherwise, the end will catch on your sleeve and spill the ink; a lens with a magnification of from 3 to 5 diameters, to show you what is right or wrong with your nib; a scrap of linen cloth to wipe it clean; and a fairly hard pencil and a ruler, preferably metric, for the marking of guide lines.

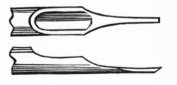

Chapter 2. TECHNIQUE

1. FREEDOM. In writing, the senses chiefly involved are sight and kinaesthesis. Though the reader uses sight alone, the writer is fully as much concerned with muscular as with visual patterns. What his hand wants to do is as important as what his eye wants to see. It is therefore obvious that in order to get the best out of materials and tools, you must understand and defer to the nature

of the hand, and the kinds of motions it performs most easily, just as much as to the nature of materials and tools themselves. Otherwise kinaesthetic images will not be able to impose themselves freely and naturally. Many of the following technical rules are primarily intended to assure this ease of action. The kinaesthetic imagination which imposes the form, the material on which it is imposed, and the tool by which it is imposed, are all, in actual practice, so firmly welded together that their activities cannot really be distinguished. All these causes work together for their common end—the production of good, true and beautiful letters.

2. COMFORT. When you write you should be comfortable at work, though not so comfortable as to give you the feeling that your work requires no effort. You should not, on the one hand, be distracted from attention to your job by discomfort, nor, on the other, be lulled by softness into a passive or sloppy attitude of mind. Sit squarely and upright in front of your desk, and with both feet on the floor. If you are not in right relation to the paper, move it on the board; do not move yourself. Be sure that your light is good. Strong daylight, either reflected from the sky, or, if the sun would otherwise shine directly on the work, diffused through a cloth or large piece of white paper, is the best for writing. Direct sunlight is too strong. No artificial light is as good as the best daylight. This is shown by comparing careful lettering done under the best natural and the best artificial lights.

3. INCLINATION. Do not write on a flat table, for this tends to make you stoop or slouch, the writing is foreshortened, and the ink flows too freely. Use the inclined board or desk. At first you will no doubt prefer an inclination of 45° with the horizontal, or even less, but an angle of between 50° and 60° is better, and you will become used to it. With such a steep angle the pen can he held nearly horizontally, and at a proper angle with the paper. The ink flows most easily and evenly and can be controlled by raising or dropping the upper end of the pen slightly. Remember that the pen is so made as to give a proper flow of ink in this position. Therefore, if you hold it with the nib downwards, the ink will drop out and make blots on your work or clothing.

THE WRITING OF LETTERS

4. LEVELS AND CANTS. Decide for yourself what distance above the floor you find most convenient for the writing level, and having so decided, stick to that level. Raise your paper under the tape or rubber band as you finish each line, so as to maintain it. Even when trying your pen on a scrap of paper, do this at the correct level. An imaginary horizontal line at this level is called the *writing level line*. Do not confuse this term with the *writing line*, which is the mark actually ruled on the paper as a guide for the letters. These two lines normally coincide, but sometimes, to make certain kinds of letters more conveniently, you may *cant* the paper somewhat, and then the *writing line* and *writing level line* are no longer coincident. For those who are left-handed a left cant is almost a necessity. If for a certain alphabet you find a cant convenient, establish it definitely in your mind, and use it whenever you write that alphabet. Otherwise the practice of canting the paper may easily degenerate into mere laxity.

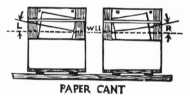

PAPER CANT

5. HANDS. Hold the pen so that the nib is a little below the other end, the shaft making a slight angle with the horizontal. This angle, shown at A, is called the pen's *elevation*. The lateral angle of the shaft with the writing line is the pen's *direction*. This should vary between 60° and 80°. B shows pen direction, but the angle is distorted because it is not seen directly from above, but from the viewpoint of the writer. Rest the heel of the hand lightly on the board, the thumb and two first fingers holding the reed firmly, and the others relaxed. Do not press enough to spread the nib even slightly, but let it move gently and evenly over the surface, with both corners bearing equally. A tight grip will destroy the quality of the kinaesthetic images, will make it impossible to feel what the nib is doing, and may even cause a splutter of ink by stubbing one corner into the paper. The aim of the beginner should be a uniform lightness of touch. Few students are willing at first to hold the spatula in the left hand, but it is essential to do so. It is not only necessary in keeping the paper firmly against the pad, but its use tends to keep the writer's body squarely in front of his work and helps him to keep his place. For left-handed writers it is obvious that the pen and spatula change hands.

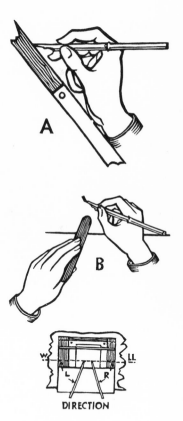

DIRECTION

47

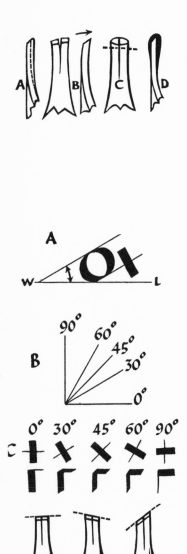

6. CARE OF NIB. Keep your pen sharp, and keep it clean. You cannot make good letters with a dull or dirty pen. If the thin lines begin to lose their crispness, your pen needs resharpening. A shows bluntness of the bevel which can often be cured by taking a shaving off the underneath of the nib. C shows bluntness of the skew, to cure which you must make a new transverse cut. If the nib of a quill tends to spread, this can often be corrected by pressing in the direction of the arrow, as at B. If gummy ink begins to clog it, take out the spring, and clean it thoroughly. If you keep the ink bottle stoppered it will keep thin longer. Keep ink off the back of the nib, for this causes a drop to form at the tip (D), and clean thins cannot be made until this is wiped off. This is why, in calligraphy, a pen is always filled rather than dipped. A calligraphic tool, like a duck, should have a wet belly and a dry back.

7. PEN SLANT. The angle between the thin edge of the nib, and therefore the thin stroke it makes, and the writing line, is the *Pen Slant* (A). It may be expressed in degrees (B), or by a pen-made cross (C), the thin stroke of which makes the particular angle with the writing line. C shows these crosses for five different pen slants, typical of the infinite number of angles which may be drawn within a quadrant. With the 0° pen slant the vertical is full width and the horizontal a hair line. With the 30°, 45°, and 60° pen slants, the verticals are respectively a little thicker, the same width, and a little thinner, than the horizontals. With the 90° pen slant the vertical is a hair line and the horizontal of full thickness. Letters written with 0° pen slant are called *straight pen* letters. Those written with pen slants of 30° and 45° are examples of *slanted pen* letters. Both these kinds are of the greatest importance in calligraphy. The last two groups, 60° and 90° angles, have little practical use, and are seldom seen. Though many of the other angles we have mentioned may effect pen slant, far the most important is skew. D, E, and F show three skews. In D the nib is cut off square, and the natural direction of the shaft causes a slanting pen letter. The skew at E makes for straight pen letters. F is cut for a left-handed writer, and, with the help of a left cant to the paper, can be used to make either straight pen or slanted pen letters.

48

THE WRITING OF LETTERS

8. EYE AND HAND. We have pointed out that writing uses both kinaesthetic and visual senses, and that the effects of the former on letters are omissions, roundness, extension of verticals, compression, tilt and slope. It is time to contrast with these qualities a corresponding set which the eye tends to impose upon letters. These are completeness in letters, the clear distinction of straight from curved lines, evenness of height, full circles, verticality of solid strokes, and verticality in the axes of circles. If you think about these two contrasted lists of qualities you will see that the slanting pen position is suited to the production of the first, and the straight pen position to the second. In the slanting pen position the hand is satisfied somewhat at the expense of the eye, and this accounts for the popularity of slanting pen letters with most scribes. With the straight pen, the eye is satisfied but the hand is inconvenienced, and this accounts for the value of this position as a discipline, for the hand is trained by dominance over it of the eye, until true kinaesthetic forms have been developed. Here are the cursive and visual tendencies compared to each other.

The Hand Tends to	*The Eye Tends to*
1. Omit parts.	1. Keep all parts.
2. Round parts.	2. Distinguish curves and straights.
3. Extend verticals.	3. Keep heights even.
4. Compress circles.	4. Keep circles full.
5. Tilt vertical strokes.	5. Keep strokes vertical.
6. Slope axes of compressed curves.	6. Keep axes vertical.
These tendencies suit	*These tendencies suit*
7. Slanted pen position.	7. Straight pen position.

1. DIRECTION AND SEQUENCE. The eye reads but the hand writes. The eye does not see a record of all the strokes the hand makes, but only those where the pen touches the paper. In rapid writing, the usually invisible kinaesthetic patterns tend to leave a trace. If the strokes of the whole pattern are written in the proper sequence, the resulting cursives are still legible, because they resemble our small letters which were developed from the capitals by means of similar stroke sequences. You should learn and always follow the logical stroke sequence for each letter as shown.

2. CAPITALS. This plate shows the result of following the corrected skeletons with a pen slant of about 30°. It is in general a good, clear alphabet. The plate also shows the round forms, and the Arabic numerals, written with the same pen. But among these twenty-six letters there are two that have not the same general weight or color as the rest. N, composed of two strong verticals and an even stronger diagonal, is a trifle heavier than the other letters. Z, composed of two weak horizontals and a still weaker diagonal, is definitely light in color. These defects are overcome by changing the pen slant slightly for the verticals in N and the diagonal in Z, thus diminishing what is over-thick, and strengthening what is over-thin.

3. SERIFS. But if once we begin to modify this alphabet, Plate VII, there is no reason why we should stop here. The letters with single verticals springing from the lower writing line, F, I, P, T, and Y, look slightly unstable, and we give them a straight stroke by way of a foot. To preserve a reasonable unity these serifs are not only also added as feet to H, K, M, N, R, U, and X, but to the top of the other vertical of N, and to the tops of diagonals in K, V, W, X and Y.

4. TRIANGULAR HEADS. The strengthening of the lower writing line with these stabilizing serifs tends to make the tops of verticals standing alone look weak. To reinforce them with horizontal serifs would be monotonous, and so we finish them with the triangular head. This termination is as characteristic a slanted pen shape as is the straight serif itself, and the use of the two together

50

combines the design advantages of unity and variety. The triangular head is made in three strokes: 1, a thin diagonal from lower left to upper right, stopping at what will be the top of the finished letter: 2, the main vertical, a thick stroke directly downwards; and 3, a thick curve, starting from the same position as stroke 1, and swinging around into stroke 2. If the triangle is not solid black, make it so with the tip of the nib. A variant on the triangular head substitutes a horizontal to the right for the first stroke, 2 and 3 being the same.

5. SWASHES. Thick downward diagonal strokes, curving toward the lower end, are called *swash strokes*. They occur in the tails of K, Q, and R. This is an easy stroke for the pen and hand to execute. You can also begin such strokes with a similar curve.

6. SMALL LETTERS. Plate VIII shows the result of writing the small letter skeleton with a slanting pen. Like the corresponding capitals, this is a good clear alphabet. As with them, the strokes of the small letters may end in serifs and triangular heads. We show both forms of a and g, but put the more elaborate first because these were developed by the slanting pen, and are suited to it.

7. ENDINGS. The first development, Plate IX, is to strengthen the weakness of all ascenders and descenders, and the tops which stand alone of i, j, and u, by giving them triangular heads. Some other stroke endings, such as the tops of c, f, and s, are given delicacy by adding *fine strokes* or short *tip flourishes*. These endings are made by rotating the pen towards the writer when the square end of the stroke is reached, and then extending the stroke with the tip or corner of the nib in continuation of the main curve. The roundness of the skeletons of the small letters makes a round type of termination a fitting development. Some of these, as in l and t, are so important that we consider them parts of the skeletons themselves. These we call *hooks*. Other round endings we consider merely as pen developments, and call *beaks*.

8. FORMAL VARIANTS. Variants are made by substituting straight serifs for beaks. These, because slightly less cursive, have a little more dignity and formality. We show i, l, and t as examples, but it is of course understood that if straight serifs are used at all,

51

ABCDEFGHIJ
KLMNOPQR
STUVWXYZ&

ABCDEFGHIJ
KLMNOPQR
STUVWXYZ&
ðeghmu
1234567890

VI. SLANTING PEN CAPITALS

52

ABCDEFGHIJ
KLMNOPQR
STUVWXYZ

‖‖⌐⌐⌐⌐⌐⌐CAM·
ANWMBJK
DEGQRS·&

deghmtu
1234567890

VII. WITH ENDINGS

53

abcdefghij

klmnopqr

stuvwxyz

agilt

1234567890

VIII. SLANTING PEN SMALL

54

abcdefghij
klmnopqr
stuvwxyz
agilt

1234567890

IX. WITH ENDINGS

55

abcdefghijk
lmnopqrs
tuvwxyz
agkvwy
aefghkmxy

X. ITALIC SMALL

56

ABCDEFG

HIJKLMN

OPQRSTU

VWXYZ·&

1234567890

XI. ITALIC CAPITALS

they must be substituted for beaks consistently throughout the alphabet. An exception is the numeral 1, which is almost invariably given a triangular head.

9. ITALICS. Plate X shows the Italic skeleton written with a slanting pen and developed similarly to the small letters of Plate IX. Italics are often written with a greater pen slant than small letters, sometimes as much as 45°. Regular slanted pen capitals may be used with small Italics, or slanted pen capitals which have been given a slight tilt. But as a relief from the monotony of small Italics, the capitals used with them, Plate XI, are often written with greater exuberance and freedom, showing particularly in the flourished endings. Such capitals are, however, obviously unsuited for use without small letters.

10. CURSIVE WRITING. If Italics are written rather small, with a dipped rather than a filled pen, on a slight rather than a great inclination, we get the typical informal hand of our tradition at its best. We show here examples of the rapid writing of a few contemporary penmen, and a diagram which shows how speed simplifies stroke sequence. Strokes to the left and upward, which are rare in formal hands, become common as letters are written rapidly with the pen almost always touching the paper. In such informal writing there is no need to use a special alphabet of cursive capitals. Roman capitals, written freely with the pen, are more legible than the rounded forms that have been used for informal initials for the last few generations.

Chapter 4. STRAIGHT PEN

1. CAPITALS. Plate XII shows the result of following the corrected skeletons with a straight pen. The disadvantages in the distribution of weight are at once obvious. The horizontals are little more than hair lines, the verticals are thick, and the diagonals of equal weight in both directions. The weakness of the horizontals can be corrected in two ways. They may be actually thickened by a slight turning of the pen, or as in Plate XIII their ends may be emphasized by the addition of serifs, and the strokes thus apparently

58

strengthened. The serif at the end of a thin horizontal is made in four strokes, rotating the pen as for tip flourishes. Because the second swings off like the spur of a railroad track, this ending is called the *spur serif*. The lower diagram shows how to make a double spur serif. Make both of these serifs quickly, allowing the ink to fill the outlines while they are still wet. The balanced weight of the diagonal strokes is varied by turning the pen to a slanting position, and attention may be diverted from their thickness by leading the eye out in various delicate elaborations. Swashes, acute triangular heads, and tip flourishes, help to lighten the appearance of the heavy strokes in many of the letters. The dot, in order to give it vertical balance, is made with the pen turned to a slant of 45°.

2. ROUND FORMS. The round variants are so well suited to the straight pen that we have included them in the alphabet as typical straight pen forms. These should be used with restraint, however, as their unfamiliarity may make their meaning obscure to some readers. The Arabic numerals are also well suited to the straight pen, by reason of their many curves.

3. SMALL LETTERS. Plate XIV gives the small skeleton written with the straight pen, and showing the same faults as do the corresponding capitals—horizontals too thin, verticals thick, and diagonals balanced in weight. But there is a new fault also. The thin part of the letter body in a, b, d, etc. is on the body's vertical axis, and therefore at some distance from the heavy vertical stroke. The curved stroke, thin at the bottom of the body, thickens rapidly as it nears the vertical. When this thick curve and the thick vertical meet, there appears a heavy spot, or accent of strength, which is a serious defect in this alphabet. If this heavy junction could be lightened, as if a shallow inverted V cut were made in the bottom of it, the letter would be much improved. This effect can be produced by drawing out the vertical into a beak at the bottom, this beak balancing the rising curve coming into the vertical on the other side. This device adds a pleasant cursive quality, and relieves, as with a series of little white waves, what would otherwise be a flatness on the writing line. The same problem, when it occurs at the top of some of these letters, is solved in the same way.

ABCDÐEƐF

FGHⱣIJKL·

MⱮNOPP

QꝖRSTUᴆ

VWXYZ&

1234567890

XII. STRAIGHT PEN CAPITALS

60

ABCDDEE

FFGHHIJK

LMMNOP

PQQRSTU

UVWXYZ&

1234567890

XIII. WITH ENDINGS

61

abcdefgh
ijklmnop
qrstuvw
wxyyz
1234567890

XIV. STRAIGHT PEN SMALL

abcdefgh

ijklmnop

qrstuvw

uwxyyz

1234567890

XV. WITH ENDINGS

4. LIGATURES. The formality and strictness of the straight pen position calls for a further relief, Plate XV, in the direction of cursiveness. This is achieved by a development of the beak, called the *ligature*. The ligatures are of two kinds, round and square. The first is somewhat like a hook in appearance, but it passes its thinnest point and becomes thicker as it attaches, or binds itself to, the succeeding letter. The square ligatures occur in letters which end in a vertical stroke not tied back to the body. The square ligature leaves its vertical at a right angle instead of in a curve. It gives a little more formality to the letters it adorns, and a variety to the manuscript as a whole. Thus a has a curved ligature, but n a square one.

5. PULLED CURVES. When certain letters, as c and e, are connected with those following them by ligatures, they tend to collide with them unless something is done to prevent it. To allow clearance at the tops, while the bottoms are connected, you can give the axis of such a letter a slight backward slope. This is called giving the letter a *pulled curve*. By means of pulling curves a great evenness in weight can be achieved in straight pen writing. When the hand becomes accustomed to pulling the curves of c and e, there is also a slight tendency to the same back slope in the other curved forms.

CHAPTER 5. PEN CONSTRUCTION

1. TWO METHODS. A letter may be thought of in two distinct ways, either as a skeleton, or as a surface. Either we think of the axes of the strokes as the important elements of a letter, or we think of its boundaries. Corresponding to these points of view are two methods by which letters may be made. In the first, the hand guides the writing tool along the skeletons, and the tool enriches these with thicks and thins. In the second, the mind sees an image having the property of area, and the hand draws the boundaries of these areas. The first is the *direct* method, and produces *written* letters. The second is the method of *construction*, and produces *drawn* letters.

64

2. DIRECT PLAIN. Letters made by a uniform thickening of skeletons we call *Plain Letters*, in preference to *sans serifs*, the more usual term. *Direct Plain* letters may be made with the round nibbed metal pens described earlier, such letters forming a transition between marking and true writing. The ends of the strokes of these letters are round. Plain letters may also be made with a writing pen by changing the pen slant to keep a uniform thickness in all strokes. These we call *Graphic Plain* letters. They are a variety of true writing, and the ends of the strokes are more or less square.

3. CONSTRUCTED PLAIN. The most rigorous Plain letters are constructed with mechanical drawing instruments. Since the skeletons are corrected, compasses cannot make all the curved outlines, and a French curve will be found unavoidable. These we call *Mechanical Plain* letters. If the letters are drawn free hand with a crowquill, the outlines of the straight strokes will naturally be slightly concave, and this quality marks these as *Free Hand Plain* letters. In either case, as soon as you begin constructing letters from the outside, you will meet the problem of ending the strokes. How will you finish the top of A, flat or in a point? Will you cut off the feet of A square or horizontally? The only rule is to apply consistently to the whole alphabet whatever principle you adopt.

4. BUILT–UPS. If the image in the mind is of a letter with thicks and thins, and is materialized with a small writing tool like a quill, you get a letter which has the graphic quality of thick and thin strokes, outlined with flat concave arcs. Such letters are usually also imagined with serifs, and these too take the form of flat arcs. These are called *Built-ups*. The springy and elastic quality of their strokes gives them a delicacy and lightness which prevents their size from oppressing smaller written letters with which they are used. The images may be either those of straight or slanting pen forms, but it is interesting to notice the great preference of experienced scribes for the former. In Built-ups, the graphic reasons for slanting pen letters no longer apply, and the visual regularity of the straight pen forms make these almost universally popular. Plate XVIII shows an alphabet of Built-up capitals, and the strokes by which they are outlined, separated from each other.

ABCDEFGHI
JKLMNOPQR
STUVWXYZ
1234567890

ABCDEFGHI
JKLMNOPQR
STUVWXYZ
1234567890

XVI. DIRECT & GRAPHIC PLAIN

66

ABCDEFGHI
JKLMNOPQR
STUVWXYZ
1234567890

ABCDEFGHI
JKLMNOPQR
STUVWXYZ
1234567890

XVII. MECHANICAL & FREE HAND PLAIN

ABCDEFG
HIJKLMN
OPQRSTU
VWXYZ&
OBS·K·
deghm

XVIII. BUILT-UP LETTERS

5. FILLING IN. Plain and Built-up letters are not imagined as outlines, but as surfaces whose outlines may be drawn. So as soon as you draw the outline, fill it in with the same ink, and before the outline is dry. Fill in very thin outlines with a brush with a delicate point. For quill-drawn letters with thicker outlines, use the quill itself. For constructing very large letters use a brush both for drawing and filling in. Letters may, of course, be imagined as areas of the same color as the writing surface, and if you so conceive them, you will fill in the spaces around the letters rather than the letters themselves. This is not, however, a practical way of making pen or brush letters, so we merely mention its theoretical possibility, and the fact that it is common in other techniques, such as engraving on metal. Its advantage is that it tends to make the letters an integral part of the object they adorn. And just as it is easy to write in other colors than black, so letters may be drawn and filled with a variety of hues. As water color flows less freely from the pen than ink, lower the board when using it. For the printer it is expensive to use more than one color, but for the calligrapher it is easy to enrich his work in this way.

6. TECHNIQUE. Just as mechanical marking tools make Mechanical Plain letters, and free marking tools Free Hand Plain letters, so the pen that outlines the thick and thin strokes of Built-ups makes lines which have something of the same quality. The quill is cut with an extra long slit, used without a spring, and on a board only slightly inclined. As the images will be straight pen forms, this drawing quill should be held in the straight pen position. If you keep your eye on the space between the outlines you will find it a better guide to regularity than the lines themselves. Draw the inside lines of curved strokes first. The straight pen position will make thin parts of curves and horizontal serifs as thin strokes, but to emphasize the greater importance of horizontal strokes that are parts of the skeleton, turn the pen sidewise when making them. This also leaves the pen ready to make a serif at the end of the horizontal member. At the widening of curved strokes, as at the upper end of C, you use both pen positions, the upper outline being a hair line and the lower, the full thickness of the nib.

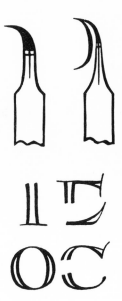

69

7. QUILLS FOR BUILT–UPS. You may make the long slit by cutting directly down on the back of the quill as we show in the margin. This is an old method of splitting a quill and if you prefer to shape your pen first you may split it afterwards in this way. For built-ups, as for writing, you must learn to examine the nib frequently with a strong lens.

8. SMALL LETTERS. Small Plain letters are constructed in the same way as capitals. The skeletons are widened until sufficiently heavy with uniformity in small Mechanical Plain letters, and with a certain flat concavity in the outlines of small Free Hand Plain letters. For small Built-ups, first understand the written exemplars, whether straight pen, slanting pen, or Italics, and then draw similar shapes with a quill. Numerals can, of course, be constructed in the same ways.

9. DANGERS. The main difference between written and drawn letters is not in the materials and tools used, but in the mental process by which the form is evolved, and the ways in which this is imposed. The shape of a well written letter results from following the lines of a proper skeleton with a properly made and held pen. The mind supplies the skeleton, and the tool does the rest. The technique of construction imposes less control on the designer, and therefore demands that he exercise more control over himself. He may go wrong because of false notions of skeletons, examples of which we see in contemporary *Block letters*. Here the attempt to unify the actual width of all letters results in degraded and vulgar shapes. But the specific danger of Built-ups lies in the fact that not only must the mind supply knowledge of the skeleton, but also of what happens when it is translated into graphic strokes. This knowledge can only be acquired by experience. Therefore a designer should not construct Built-ups until he has been long familiar with formal writing. Otherwise, the liberty given him by the technique of constructing will turn to license and foolishness. Until you know the meaning of a shape in terms of its primary technique, you are not free to adapt that shape to another. Building-up letters is a free way of expressing the logic of certain forms, but that logic must be a mental possession, or the letters will not be good.

BLOCK

SECTION III. *Incising*

CHAPTER 1. MATERIALS AND TOOLS

1. STONE. As stone is the most important material for the letter cutter, this section deals with it exclusively, with the exception of two paragraphs, the last in this and in the succeeding chapter. Letters cut in wood have shapes similar to those cut in stone, but the techniques by which they are made are so dissimilar that we add these two extra paragraphs. Stones differ from each other in structure and in hardness. Limestones are usually soft. Marbles are limestones which have crystallized. They vary between soft and medium in hardness. Slates are made up of thin laminations, as a book is made up of leaves, and so must be carved on the cleavage plane only. The best slates are of even color and medium hardness. Granites result from the crystallization of molten mixtures. They are usually extremely hard, and their crystal pattern is made up of different minerals.

2. SPECIAL STONES. Among American stones Indiana Limestone is good, being soft to cut, but hard enough to withstand the climate. Among the best of the white marbles is Yule Colorado, though some of the harder grades of Vermont marble may equal it. The southern marbles, as Tennessee and Georgia, have in general larger crystals and are harder than the northern varieties. Dark gray Monson Maine slate is one of the most durable of stones, but it is easy to carve and its close texture makes it possible to cut the most delicate letters. Colored slates have various properties that make them less satisfactory, especially for exterior inscriptions. Foreign limestones and marbles nearly always weather badly in our climate. A safe general rule is to avoid all foreign stones for exterior use.

3. CHISELS. Stone is cut with steel chisels driven with mallet or hammer. The chisels most used have square ends, but skew chisels are convenient for special purposes. The bevel is steep for the soft (A), and more obtuse for the hard stones (B). The cutting edge is tempered to a pigeon-wing blue for the soft stones, copper color for the medium, and straw color for the hard granites. You can judge

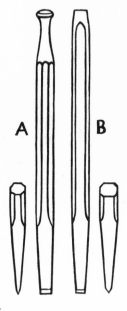

71

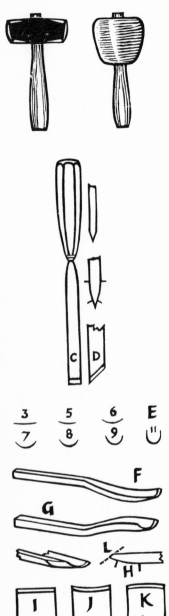

the hardness of a chisel by the way in which it rubs on the sharpening stone. The heads of chisels are of two sorts, adapted either for use with mallets (A), or hammers (B).

4. HAMMERS. Both the iron hammers and wooden mells of the letterer should be small, as heavy blows are not needed. For small letters in soft stone a wooden mell of one pound is good. For larger letters in soft stone, the wooden mell should not exceed two pounds. For any lettering in a hard stone an iron hammer of one pound is sufficiently heavy.

5. OTHER TOOLS. As the edge of a chisel is first sharpened by hammering and filing it on an anvil, and then tempered, you will need a small forge, if you are going to cut letters in a serious way; but while you are a beginner, a blacksmith or tool maker can do this work for you. To keep your chisels sharp you must have a water grindstone, oil stones, and an oil can filled with kerosene. For laying out inscriptions you should have tracing paper, carbon paper, a large wooden square and a straight edge, and a stylus. For the surfacing of stones you will need an assortment of abrasives and grits. Any letter carver can advise you where to buy these materials and tools in your neighborhood. If you carve hard stones professionally you should protect your health by wearing a respirator. This is not necessary for occasional carving in hard stones, nor for any amount of carving in marble and limestone.

6. WOOD TOOLS. Letters are incised in wood with chisels and gouges, but usually without a mallet. Both should have wooden handles, octagonal to prevent their rolling off the bench. The bevel of both varies from acute for the softer to obtuse for the harder woods. #1 chisels have square ends (C); and #2, skewed ends (D). As curves are incised in wood by cutting *into* the surface with a gouge of about the sweep of the cut to be made, you will need many gouges, one for every kind of curve; but it is better to get them only as you need them. We show the sweeps of some wood gouges with their standard numbers (E). Most gouges have straight shanks, but for carving under awkward conditions, there are also *front bent* (F), and *back bent* (G), gouges. A hard Pike Arkansas oil stone is good for rubbing up the edge. Always keep the tool at

72

the same angle so as to keep the end square and the bevel flat, but you may later round the shoulder of the bevel, (H), so as to be able to use the tool quite flat, in the cutting of backgrounds for raised letters. The cutting edge, looked at from the top, should be square (I), or slightly concave (J), never convex (K). Gouges cut best when ground with a short inside bevel (L), and for this you will need a variety of slip stones each with a convex edge exactly fitted to the sweep of the gouge, and a wooden vise (M), to hold them in.

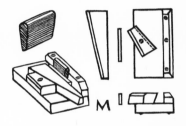

Chapter 2. TECHNIQUE

1. GENERAL ADVICE. Keep the stone horizontal and about the height of your belt. Ultimately the ideal is to carve letters *in situ*, and this usually means a vertical surface, but the beginner must learn by carving horizontal surfaces first. Put the stone where you can walk all around it, and thus work from whatever direction is convenient. Learn to use chisel and hammer in either hand. If you practice this from the start, it is not too difficult, and there will be occasions later where it will be invaluable.

2. CHISEL ANGLE. For soft stones hold the chisel at an angle of about 45° to the surface. The harder the stone the nearer the vertical you must hold the chisel. A common mistake for beginners is to hold the chisel too flat.

3. RHYTHM. What gets the work done is not heavy pounding, but a rapid and rhythmical series of light, well directed blows. Even in granite, a deft snap of the wrist is more effective than a heavy blow from the shoulder. For slate this rhythm is often very rapid, and results in an orderly series of chisel marks across the cut, which give it an agreeable texture, and speak of the means by which it was produced.

4. PRACTICE. Your first task is to find out what the technique really wants to do, and why V cuts are its natural expression. Mark on a stone surface a pattern of lines of all sorts, and develop these lines as V cuts, until you have some success with an even, fairly rapid rhythm of light blows.

73

PLAIN

GLYPTIC

ROMAN

5. PLAIN LETTERS. Next, draw Plain letters,—skeletons with uniform width. Make the straight strokes first, cutting one side completely and then the other, being careful to increase the angle of the chisel as you approach the ends. Then cut the triangular planes, keeping the same angle here with the surface. In cleaning out the valleys you will tend to emphasize them, but as these are Plain letters, this tendency should be resisted as much as possible. In making curves cut the *inside* first.

6. GLYPTIC LETTERS. These triangles are the normal result of the right use of a chisel, and may, even in letters of uniform thickness of stroke, be properly developed into true serifs. Such letters, also, may well have a slight curvature in the outlines of the cuts. Due to their lack of fine detail they are suitable in large sizes for coarse and hard stones. We call them Glyptic letters.

7. ROMAN CAPITALS. When you add to such letters the graphic factor of thick and thin strokes, and allow the serif to de-velop still further, you get true Roman Capitals. In these the curves are not only carved first from the inside, but from the thin to the thick. Because a cut gets deeper as it gets thicker, there is danger of getting it too thick and too wide at the point where it should begin again to diminish in depth and width. Therefore, turn your chisel in at the thick part of the curved cut. The little triangles can be cleaned out after the main cuts are finished.

8. GLYPTIC TENDENCIES. Carving will teach you the ad-vantages of avoiding, when possible, junctions between straight strokes and angles, as in K; and why it is reasonable to finish acute angles, as in N, in a point rather than a serif. The three main glyptic tendencies are these: the ending of straight strokes in *serifs*, acute angles in *points*, and the *avoidance of junctions* between angles and straights.

9. BRUSH LAYOUT. Roman Capitals, Small Letters and Italics may all be written directly on a stone, using water color and a lettering brush, between carefully ruled lines. These may then be developed directly with a chisel and mallet into good inscription letters. This was the method of the cutters of the great classical inscriptions, and is still the best manner of working.

74

10. PAPER LAYOUT. Unfortunately it is usually necessary to-day for the letter carver to prepare for his patron a full-size drawing of his inscription. These are the steps in making such a drawing. First, by means of small pencil sketches, determine the arrangement and sizes of the letters. Then mark the writing parallels so determined on a piece of heavy paper at full size. With brush and ink write each of the letters you will need at full size on another paper. From these brush-written letters trace each line of letters on a strip of tracing paper properly ruled. When all the lines are traced, fix the strips in their proper places on the full-size layout with rubber cement. Before this dries you will be able to adjust the spacing both within and between the lines. When all is as good as you can make it, make a single clean tracing of the whole inscription. You can transfer this drawing to the stone surface by means of carbon paper or red chalk, and in the case of soft stones scratch the letters on with a stylus. If you do not so scratch on the letters, it is better either to protect with a mask of paper the letters not actually being worked on, or to transfer only one line at a time from the full-size drawing. This whole method is so complex that unless you try to improve your letters at each step, they will become completely lifeless. Unless you try to make them better and better as you go along, they will get worse and worse.

11. DIFFERENT STONES. Every inscription must be designed to suit the nature of the stone it will be carved on. In light colored ones, such as Indiana Limestone and especially the white marbles, the lighted side of a V cut looks so much like the surface that, at a short distance, only the shadow side of the cut counts, and therefore the letters must be designed much wider than looks well in a drawing. In marbles and slates of close grain and even color, the serifs can be designed much more delicately than in coarser stones which call for simpler treatment. Stones with large crystals, particularly if, as in granite, these are of different minerals, need letters big and bold enough to dominate the pattern. Avoid high polish on marbles and granites. Stone surfaces are smoothed by various abrasives, a natural grit for marble, and for granite, steel shot, carborundums and hones. If you work down a natural split surface

75

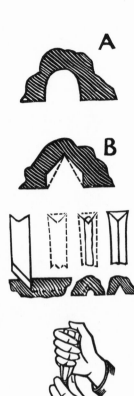

in slate by hand, first with rasps and later with abrasives, you will get a much more agreeable surface for lettering than the dead flat plane produced by the mechanical rubbing bed.

12. MISTAKES. The average V cut is not as deep as it looks, and mistakes in cutting usually not as serious as they seem, unless the stone has been bruised by heavy blows. You must resurface the stone over an area large enough to escape notice and then recut all the letters so erased. If possible, this area should include one edge of the stone, particularly on a dead flat surface.

13. COLOR AND GOLD. Sometimes legibility demands the painting or gilding of incised letters. For color, shellac the cuts and the surrounding surface, and then paint the cuts with dry color mixed with spar varnish. For gilding use shellac in the same way, and finish the cuts with size and gold leaf. Clean up the surface with the appropriate abrasive. For polished marble use the soft side of cuttlefish bone.

14. FANTASTIC SECTIONS. Designers of inscriptions frequently show on their drawings sections quite unrelated to the realities of incising. Those shown in the margin can be cut by hand, but will take three to five times as much labor as the normal V. A can only be made by cutting *into* the stone rather than *along* it. B is produced by first cutting a deep V, and then two other valleys in it, a labor unrewarded by any extra excellence in the letter.

15. WOOD TECHNIQUE. To incise straight strokes, begin by cutting each serif valley directly into the wood with a skew chisel. Next, rough out the stroke with a #11 gouge of the correct size, sharp enough to cut across the grain. Then with a chisel clean up the strokes to a V, as in a stone letter. For curves, make the *outside* cut first, using a gouge a little quicker than the outline to be cut, and then the inner cut, using a gouge a little flatter than the line. Hold the gouge as shown at C, cut *down* at the angle of the V, moving the tool around in the directions shown, so as not to misuse the grain.

Chapter 3. CHISEL CONSTRUCTION

1. LINES AND SURFACES. We can think of letters to be made with a chisel in the same two ways in which we think of letters to be made with a pen or a brush. Either the skeletons or the outlines may be of chief importance in our minds. If the imagined strokes have breadth, we may see the letters in our minds either as Plain letters or as letters with thicks and thins.

2. TWO METHODS. If with your chisel you simply follow a skeleton, you will get an incised letter. But if you outline the strokes of a letter with it, you will get an incised constructed letter. This is chisel construction. In the example the directly incised I is made with one cut, and the constructed I with four.

3. SUNK LETTERS. Letters are seldom imagined as incised outlines merely, but as sunk letters or letters in relief. If the space between the cuts is cleaned away to a new plane, we get sunk letters. Because they tend to be clumsy, such letters are rarely used, and then generally for very large inscriptions. The space between the cuts is sometimes left convex rather than flat, and this treatment is known as *pillowing*. In large letters the pillow may be gilded. If you do this, do not gild the sides of the cuts, and be sure that the top of the pillow is below the stone surface. After gilding you can clean the sides of the cuts with the chisel, and rub the surfaces down without injuring the gold leaf.

4. RELIEF LETTERS. If the background outside the incised outlines is cut back to a new plane we get relief letters. They are often suitable for purposes of special formality or emphasis. Because small letters and italics are informal and compact, these are not suited to carving in relief. But Plain and Roman Capitals are often so carved with good effect when the words are of particular importance. They are usually more legible than V cut letters of the same size. A common mistake is to carve them in too high relief. $\frac{1}{8}$ or $\frac{3}{16}$ of an inch is sufficient in most cases.

77

PART C. PURPOSE
CHAPTER 1. LEGIBILITY OF LETTERS

1. LEGIBILITY. It is the function of letters to be understood. Legibility is their general purpose. The particular purpose of any given example of lettering is legibility within the particular conditions under which it is to be read. Among other variables which affect the legibility of letters are the size, weight, and proportions of the letters themselves; the relationships between them; the nature of the surface; and the conditions under which the surface is seen, such as the strength of the light and the angle from which it is viewed.

2. LEGIBLE PARTS. Legible letters are made up of legible parts legibly arranged. The *parts* are the solid strokes of the letters and the voids within and around them. Good *arrangement* is the proper handling of these solids and voids in relation to each other. It consists in a judicious balance of likeness and unlikeness among the parts—a proper degree of uniformity, combined with a proper degree of diversity—in both the solids and the voids.

3. THE STROKE. You cannot understand the solids of letters unless you understand their simplest unit which is the stroke—a line given thickness by being materialized with a tool. The thickness of the stroke varies with different techniques. In Plain letters, by definition, all strokes have equal thickness, their standard being that of the letter I. In Graphic letters, strokes vary in thickness from hair lines to those of full breadth, and the width of the pen or brush is the standard that determines the variation. In Built-up letters, strokes vary in thickness as do the Graphic letters on which their shapes are based, but the standard of both thicks and thins is in the mind.

4. DIRECTIONS. You cannot make a stroke without giving it *some* direction, and as legibility depends on the characters of skeletons, you must make these directions the right ones. This is particularly the case in the distinction between straights and curves. Unless you keep the straights true, the curves full, and the relationships between them distinct, your letters will not be fully legible.

78

5. WEIGHT. You cannot make a stroke without giving it *some* weight. The proper weight of strokes is that which gives the greatest legibility to the letters they compose. The breadth of such a stroke should be a mean somewhere between illegible extremes—the extreme of thinness on the one hand and the extreme of thickness on the other. The extremely thin stroke is illegible because it tends to actual invisibility; the extremely thick because it tends to destroy the character of the letter. In the diagram, the round dot and the solid triangle still suggest O and A because the outlines of these letters are characteristic, but N and Z tend to be indistinguishable from each other as they approach solid squares. If we make the thickness of the horizontals of a Plain E equal to the spaces between them, we have strokes whose breadth is one-fifth of the letter height. This gives a logical maximum breadth of solids for Plain letters in which all strokes are of exactly the same thickness.

6. LETTER UNIFORMITY. If you determine your directions accurately, and give these directions suitable weight by the proper technical methods, the letters will have a family likeness which will itself be a source of legibility. The blackened parts of the letters shown are similar to each other because they are arrived at in similar ways. In good writing, the nature of the pen, the way in which it is handled, and the individual interpretation of the traditional skeletons all combine to give uniformity to the letters. Look after the principles and the results will look after themselves.

7. LETTER DIVERSITY. To avoid confusing particular letters with each other, you should emphasize their most characteristic parts. Thus to avoid confusion between P and R, the tail of the R is usually emphasized at the expense of the head; while the head of the P may be made larger than that of R. C and G may be distinguished by exaggerating the beard of the latter, and the lack of the beard in the former, by putting a serif on its upper termination, but none on its lower. Q and the round form of D are distinguished from each other, and from O, by emphasis upon their tails. When letters are flourished and treated in an ornate and exuberant way, it is these characteristic parts which should be exaggerated, for by so doing, there is the least danger of confusion.

79

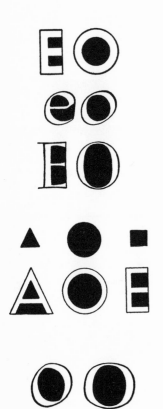

ligatures

8. THE WORD. Legible letters will not make legible words unless they are legibly related to one another. The ligature is a solid stroke which may be used to help this relationship. Graphic letters are often connected by ligatures, and thus form solid words.

Chapter 2. LEGIBILITY OF SPACES

1. LEGIBLE PARTS. The voids within and between letters are parts just as necessary to legibility as are the solid strokes themselves. Solids and voids are the complements of each other. Good arrangement among voids depends upon a judicious balance between uniformity and diversity just as it does among solids. The voids within letters are known as counters.

2. THE COUNTER. A single vertical stroke cannot define a space, but the addition to it of horizontals, as in E, inevitably does so. The spaces thus defined are typical of two-storied letters. The largest counter is that of the one-storied O, and is a convenient standard for relating spaces within and between letters. Among the small letters as among the capitals, e and o establish the limits of counter size. Different techniques affect the relations of counters to the outlines of their letters. In Plain letters the shape of counter and outline are the same. In Graphic letters they are not the same, due to the action of the writing tool. In Built-up letters this is also true, but the mind rather than the tool is the guide.

3. SHAPES. Bad letters almost always have bad counters. As the characteristic shapes of letters are triangles, circles, and squares, the letters, to be legible, must have counters which express accurately these shapes. In Plain letters the counter of A is a triangle, of O, a circle, and the counters of E, squares. In Graphic and Built-up letters these shapes are modified by the writing tool, either actually used or imagined, but they are nevertheless logical and definite shapes which must be exactly made. The typical example is the counter of the Graphic O, which, though not circular, is a logical expression of the circle, in terms of thicks and thins. Compare the angularity of the slanting pen counter with the roundness of the corresponding straight pen form.

80

4. AREAS. You cannot enclose a space with strokes without making a counter. The best size for a counter is that which gives greatest legibility to the letter—the too small counter tending toward a characterless solid, and the too large tending to reduce the stroke to invisibility. When a letter has more than one counter, as M, legibility calls for a rough equality in their areas, and it is to achieve this that its verticals are given a slight inward tilt. In the small m, the letter is properly designed if the counters are equal in weight to each other, to o, and other letters and parts of letters constructed similarly to o. The blackness of the spot made by an improperly designed m results from the neglect of this rule. This mistake can be made between letters as well as within them.

5. SPACE UNIFORMITY. Just as family likeness in solid strokes makes for uniformity, so does family likeness in the voids. In the upper word *minuscule*, an equality of weight between the counters and among the interletter spaces makes for legibility. In the lower version, m i n makes a bad spot, and there is another at the junction of u and l, and a hole between s and c which breaks the word into two pieces. The danger of spots lies chiefly in the ease with which verticals can be crowded together. The danger of holes lies chiefly in the use of letters which have not vertical sides. Remember to make the areas between letters as nearly as possible equal to each other, and to the spaces within them.

6. SPACE DIVERSITY. Diversity among the shapes of inter-letter spaces is an aid to legibility because it is a simple result of the diversity of the shapes of the letters themselves. Because the various letters differ in shape the linear distances between them must also properly vary. But as we have just seen, the areas of the inter-letter spaces must be as nearly as possible alike. To understand this we must consider again the problem of apparent width. When you can establish the apparent limits of your letters you have only to separate these limits by a uniform linear distance to have the space between the letters the same. Of course the designer does not do this mechanically in practice. The eye is always the final judge, but it becomes more sensitive when the mind understands the principles behind the phenomena which the eye sees.

81

As words
OF O

7. THE WORD SPACE. As words are the largest of the minor solids of lettering, so the spaces between them are the largest of the minor voids. To emphasize the separation between words, the spaces between them must be greater than the interletter spaces. The usual space between words is approximately that of the outside width of O.

Chapter 3. THE SHEET

1. LARGER UNITS. Words are arranged in two ways. In the first the principle of arrangement is the meaning, and because it is the function of words to convey meaning, such groupings of words we call *functional*. In the second the words are arranged with the maximum of technical convenience in mind, and these groupings we call *technical*.

2. FUNCTIONAL UNITS. Words, clauses, sentences, paragraphs, and chapters are functional. As the units become progressively larger, and the ideas they express progressively complex, the spaces between the units must also be larger, or increasingly emphasized in some other way if they are to aid the legibility of the writing. Spaces between clauses are usually somewhat greater than word spaces, and are partly occupied by strokes of punctuation. The space between sentences is usually emphasized by the use of a capital initial. The beginning of the paragraph is either indented, or marked with a still larger capital, or paragraphs are separated from each other by an empty horizontal space, a full letter line high.

3. TECHNICAL UNITS. The line, as such, is not limited by any thought to be conveyed, but by the width of the sheet and the width of its vertical margins. The text, as such, is governed by the height of the sheet, of the horizontal margins, and the number of the lines.

4. THE SHEET. The first technical unit to be considered is the sheet. It is at first a pure void, empty of all solid strokes. When the mass of lettering is built up in it, this major void is reduced to the margins.

82

5. THE LINE. Sheets are seldom wide enough, nor texts short enough, for all the letters written on them to be arranged in a single line. We therefore place the words in horizontal rows, with spaces between. With texts written all in capitals, the spaces between lines are usually a half or a whole letter height. With small letters, it is usually best to have the ends of the ascenders and descenders just clear each other. As a line of small letters is usually divided horizontally into three equal bands, this means that the space between the letter bodies will be double the height of the bodies themselves. This wide space, however, will be partly occupied by the ascenders and descenders. By writing a few lines with a large reed of suitable skew, you can easily calculate the size of letter and width of nib proper to the writing you intend to make.

6. AWKWARD BREAKS. Words are functional combinations of letters, but lines are technical combinations of words. Because, in writing, function is more important than technique, whenever the length of a line conflicts with the integrity of a word, the line must give way. Do not break a word at the end of a line when this might be confusing. Cat-ch, he-avy, and the-nce, if broken at the hyphens, might be misleading. This often raises problems for the calligrapher, which he may solve in various ways. By making some letters abnormally high or low, you can fit them together and save space. You may link them, making a single cipher for OO, as W is a single symbol for VV. You can join letters making true monograms. You may write one word above the regular line, tying it up to its proper place with a flourish. You may make certain words extra large or extra small.

7. MARGINS. Margins aid legibility by separating the lettering from distracting things around the sheet. Their combined area is usually about half that of the whole sheet, but they are of different widths, as indicated by the numbers in the diagram, which gives a good proportion. The bottom margin, by which the sheet is chiefly held, is the widest; and the top margin, the narrowest, because least important. Together, they act as a frame, which it is foolish to have too wide, but which is better too wide than too narrow. If your sheet is actually to be framed, it will obviously need less

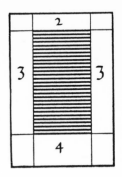

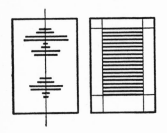

margin than otherwise. The heavier a given mass of text, the wider the margin will look in contrast to it. If you rule the vertical margin with double lines, those on the left will be guides for indentation, and those on the right will give the limits within which you must include your last letter. Because stone is more expensive to get and to work than paper or even vellum, and because stone tablets are not held in the hand to be read, their margins are usually much less than one-half of the total surface.

8. TWO ARRANGEMENTS. Just as direct lettering is making strokes with their axes in mind, and constructed lettering is making strokes with their outlines in mind, so the design of masses of letters on a rectangular sheet may be related either to the central vertical axis of the sheet, or to its edges. The first method we call *symmetrical*, and the second, *massed* arrangement.

9. MASSED ARRANGEMENT. This is a technical, rather than a functional, arrangement. Its practical advantage is that it allows the greatest amount of lettering for a given space. The available surface is as nearly as possible filled with a solid block of letters. Variety and emphasis are sacrificed to economy of space. If the lines are not equal they must be filled out with flourishes, or other strokes, to make them so. The close, even spacing and regular margins give this arrangement great richness, and thus the appeal is often to the eye, rather than to the mind. If you use small letters, they will tend to have short ascenders and descenders, and simple serifs. The strength of such an arrangement makes it necessary that any contrasts in size, weight and color of letters used with it, be correspondingly obvious and strong.

10. SYMMETRICAL ARRANGEMENT. This arrangement, on the other hand, is functional rather than technical. The lines are longer or shorter to suit the meaning to be expressed; their principle of unity lies in being balanced symmetrically on the vertical axis. The lines are not only of different lengths, but can be of different letter heights, and the ideas may be still further emphasized by the use of spaces of various heights between lines. Different kinds of letters—capitals, small letters, or italics—may be used together. The generally wider spacing of lines allows you to use

84

longer ascenders and descenders, and these may be flourished with elegance and freedom. All these contrasts are design factors in this kind of arrangement. In addition there is the contrast of large areas of the field which have no letters at all. Compared with the forthright and bold uniformity of the massed arrangement, the symmetrical tends toward elegance, fancifulness, and individuality.

11. COMBINATION ARRANGEMENTS. We distinguish these pure types of arrangement—direct and constructed, functional and technical—in order to understand the principles behind major lettering design. In actual practice most solutions are combinations, in various proportions, of massed and symmetrical arrangements. Even in the most open symmetrical sheet, lines may be grouped together to form blocks, or other patterns typical of massing. As elsewhere, each problem demands its own particular solution, and the best arrangement is that which best contributes to this solution.

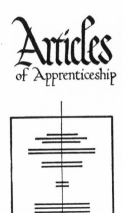

CHAPTER 4. THE BOOK

1. BOOKS. A collection of sheets of paper or vellum, folded and sewn together, is a book. Normally, all sheets, in order to be sewn together, have to be folded at least once. The size and shape of the pages of the book depend upon the size and shape of the sheets, and the number of times these are folded. If the sheet is folded only once, so as to make two pages with four writing surfaces, the book is called a *folio*. If twice, so as to become four pages with eight surfaces, it is called a *quarto*. If it is folded once again, each *signature* is made up of eight pages with sixteen surfaces, and is called an *octavo*. In this way not only the size but the relative shape of the pages is determined by the way in which the sheets are folded.

2. MARGINS. In a book, two lettered pages are usually presented to the reader at once, and except for this the principles for making margins are the same as for a single sheet. Make the inner margins about half the width of the outer. The sum of the two inner margins may be a little less than a single outside margin, but

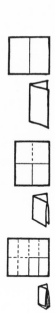

85

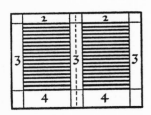

should never be more. The top margin should be between the inner and outer vertical margins in width. Keep the top very exact, as the eye detects irregularities at the upper part of a page that it overlooks at the bottom. For books that are to be bound, add an extra $\frac{1}{8}$ inch to the margins, as otherwise the binder, in trimming down the edges, may destroy the proportions you have planned. The contemporary fashion of very narrow or no margins in books has little to recommend it. The numbers in the diagram give a good relationship between margins. As in a sheet, the area should be about one-half of the whole.

3. LINES AND LETTER SIZE. The size of the letters, and therefore the number of lines on the page, is fixed by the length of the line and the number of words in it. For written books, four to eight words to a line is a good range. With more than eight, it is sometimes difficult for the eye to find the beginning of the next line. With less than four, the reader is wearied by unnecessary shifts. When you have decided the exact number of letters per line, the size of the letter is thereby determined. The height of the page and the width of the top and bottom margins now give the number of lines, and this, multiplied by the number of words per line, gives the total number of words to the page.

4. MASSED AND SYMMETRICAL PAGES. The arrangement most suitable to prose is the massed one, but books of verse may be exercises in the symmetrical method, or in a combination with many symmetrical features. Title-pages of books of all kinds are treated symmetrically. Keep the words on the title-page few, as this gives proper emphasis to ideas which should be simple, and this emphasis may be further heightened by the use of Built-up letters.

Chapter 5. PARTICULAR PURPOSES

1. TWO PATRONS. Every designer today works either for an individual patron, or for industry—a general patron. The work which leaves the calligrapher's hand is either read directly by its ultimate consumer, or is a pattern for the production of other

pieces of lettering which will eventually find many ultimate con-
sumers. You design a piece of work either for a particular person,
or as a part of the machinery of multiple production.

2. INDIVIDUAL PATRON. If you make a unique piece of
writing or incising, your problem, though difficult, is compara-
tively simple. You are in contact with your consumer, and can
ascertain his needs. Your tools are relatively simple, and you are
responsible for, and can control, the whole productive operation.

3. INDUSTRIAL PATRON. But if you make lettering for reproduction, you are not in contact with the many ultimate con-
sumers, the tools used are complex, and you are not in control of
the whole technical operation. You hand over a pattern to a group
of technicians whose job it is to reproduce it as well as they can.
If your pattern is not suited to the nature of the reproducing mech-
anisms, your work will inevitably be spoiled. Therefore you must
know all you possibly can about the reproducing techniques.

4. COMPLEXITY. The great obstacle here is the complexity of
the means of multiple production. Only by as full and intelligent
a study of the actual operations as he is able to make, will the designer be able to reduce this obstacle. It cannot be entirely removed. You can never know as much about a complicated instrument as about a simple one, and even simple instruments need a
lifetime of study. On the other hand, the more you know about
those forces that are outside your control, the more you can avoid
mistakes that you would be powerless to correct.

5. SIZE. In many reproductive techniques, the size at which you
work is not the same as that of the ultimate product. The work
that leaves your hand is of a size adjusted to your eye and to your
means of production, though the final work may be much larger or
much smaller. The change in size is taken care of by various mechanical means, often very accurate. But no matter how accurately
its shape is reproduced, a letter which is right at one size, is not
right at another. The difference between letters in 36-point type,
and the corresponding 10-point letters enlarged to the same size,
illustrates the principle. There is here a far greater impediment to
good work than is generally realized. The designer's difficulty is

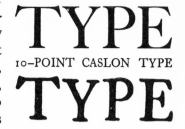

10–POINT CASLON TYPE

87

only partly removed by his use of magnifying and diminishing lenses, and photographic enlargement and reduction. It cannot be completely solved unless the patterns the designer makes are of the same size as the end product, and this is often impossible.

6. MANY MINDS. But perhaps the greatest difficulty of all lies in the fact that in industry the designer and the executor of the work are different people, and therefore much of the formal quality of the design is lost in its necessary reinterpretation by other minds, with other mental characteristics. Industry is not one great automatic mechanism which runs itself and reproduces the patterns fed into it without modification. At every point the intelligences and the wills of those who run the machines are called into play. Even if these wills and intelligences are in agreement with each other, and are as well trained, creatively, as those of the designer, they are still not *the same* as those of the designer. No man can make a good copy of another man's work. He can make a version of it either better or worse, but only a mechanism can make a true copy, and industry is not mechanical in this sense. To meet this difficulty as well as may be, you must keep your forms as simple as possible, and therefore as little liable to the distortions inherent in multiple production. The popularity of the austere shapes of Plain letters in the best industrial design is, in part at least, due to the artist's understanding of this principle.

7. SUMMARY. It is much more difficult to make patterns for industrial products of real quality, than to make the products themselves. The difficulty cannot be completely solved, but it can be partly solved if it is first understood. The solution of this problem, as of all others, depends upon a grasp of the truth concerning it. We can only design well for industry when we know what industry is. Only by understanding machines can we make industrial letters legible.

BOOK THREE

THE HISTORICAL ELEMENTS
OR
LETTERS AS THINGS TO BE LEARNED FROM

PART A. THE ANCIENT WORLD

PART B. THE MEDIEVAL WORLD

PART C. THE MODERN WORLD

THE HISTORICAL ELEMENTS
PART A. THE ANCIENT WORLD
Chapter 1. PICTURES TO LETTERS

1. COMMUNICATION. Man's intellect furnishes him with ideas, and his social nature makes it imperative that he communicate these to others of his kind. A spoken language was perhaps his first means of doing this, but it is only effective when both speaker and hearer are at the same place at the same time. Hence man needs also to be able to leave an intelligible word behind him, when he is far away.

2. PICTURES. The most primitive solution of this problem was the picture. An idea can be conveyed if a representation of some object associated with the idea can be made accurately enough to be understood. The upper drawing might be intended to mean: *The fishing is good in this part of the river*; but might easily be misread as: *the water here is full of wigglers and bad for drinking*. The second drawing is a pictograph for *thunderstorm*, but might be understood: *The third house in the row is where the magician lives*. You can see that it is practically impossible to convey more abstract ideas by means of pictures.

3. PUNS. A partial solution of the difficulty was found in the use of puns—words with one sound but with several distinct meanings. If one of the meanings of a pun is the name of a simple object which can be represented in a quick drawing, then the drawing can be understood to stand for that word, whatever its meaning may be. For example, in modern English, a drawing of a fish could stand for both the noun and the verb *fish*. Waves could represent both *sea* and *see*. A diagram of a knot could mean both *knot* and *not*. A drawing of a can could represent both a tin can or the verb for possibility. And an eye could do duty not only for *eye* but also *I* and *aye*. With such pun-signs one can write a sentence like that in the margin with some expectation that his meaning will be accurately communicated. But only a few of the many syllables of a spoken language can be so used, and this seriously limits the value of the system. If communication is to be at all free, most of the

91

puns must be rather far fetched. But in spite of these disadvantages, the ancient Mexicans and Chinese, and for centuries the Egyptians, found them not so great as to make necessary a further development toward simplicity.

4. SEMITIC LETTERS. The ancient Semites had a system of pun-signs. The word *Aleph* meant bull, and a simple picture of a bull's head stood for the sound *aleph*, in whatever meaning that sound occurred. In the same way the words, *Beth*, meaning house, *Gimmel*, meaning camel, and *Daleth*, meaning door, were represented by simple conventional signs, which stood for the sounds of the words. It occurred to someone of truly original mind that just as words can be broken down into a smaller number of syllables, so syllables can be broken down into a smaller number of more basic sounds, which can be even more simply conventionalized. This originator chose from the existing pun-signs twenty-two, suitable for his purpose, and used them to stand, not for syllables, but for their initial consonant sounds. These were true letters, though the system consisted entirely of consonants. The bull's head was no longer read *Aleph* but stood for the initial consonant of that word,—a glottal stop for which we have no equivalent. *Beth* is read B, *Gimmel*, G, *Daleth*, D, and so with the others.

5. GREEK LETTERS. When the Greeks adapted this system they found that four of the Semitic consonants did not occur in their language, and they therefore used these symbols for vowel sounds which they wanted to include. Thus *Aleph*, the bull; *He*, the window; *Yod*, the hand; and *'Ayin*, the eye, became Alpha, Epsilon, Iota, and Omicron. Two other consonants, Vau and Qoph, they used for a while as Vau and Koppa, but dropped before their system took its final form. In addition they invented five new letters of their own, bringing the total to its full development of twenty-four. They called it alpha-bet, just as we speak of learning our ABC's.

6. LATIN LETTERS. Various Italian tribes adapted the Greek alphabet to their particular needs. When one of these tribes dominated the others, and central Italy became Roman, the language

and the letter system of Rome became that of all Italian peoples. But the Roman tribe did not take over the Greek letters without change. They dropped Theta, Chi, and Omega. They kept V and Q from the primitive Vau and Koppa, which the Greeks themselves dropped. They turned the vowel Eta into a consonant as H. From Gamma or Kappa they developed G. This gave twenty-three letters.

7. ENGLISH LETTERS. The system of twenty-six which we use today is the Roman alphabet with the addition of J, U, and W. The Roman I had the value both of a consonant and a vowel. The same was true of V. The addition of J and U are a device for separating these values. J stands for the consonant use of I, the simpler straight form being reserved for the vowel use. U stands for the vowel use of V, the angular form being reserved for the consonant use. Such spellings as *loue* and *vse*, for *love* and *use*, were usual until the middle of the 17th Century. W is merely a doubling of V, and it is a mark of the essential identity of U and V that the letter which appears as a double V is still called double U.

8. DISPOSITION OF LETTERS. There are many ways of disposing letters in words and sentences besides the one with which we happen to be familiar. Semitic, Greek, and Latin peoples seem always to have arranged letters in horizontal rows, but the Chinese arrange their characters in vertical rows. We write always from left to right, but the peoples of the Near East write the other way. The primitive Greeks and Italians wrote in either direction, and sometimes in alternate directions, a method which they called Boustrophedon, or writing *as the ox plows*. Only later in the development of the Greek and Roman languages was our present convention of writing from left to right finally standardized.

9. ROMAN NUMERALS. Letters are symbols for sounds. Numerals are symbols for quantities. The Romans did not borrow the Greek number system, but had a system of their own, which is based on pictures. The sign for one is I, and, as the name *digit* suggests, was originally a picture of a finger or *digitus*. The sign for five is V, originally a representation of the hand with outstretched fingers. The other numerals have also the shapes of Latin letters, but are believed to have had a different origin, being origi-

93

nally pictures of objects associated with higher numbers. They are X for ten, L for fifty, C for a hundred, D for five hundred, and M for a thousand. These numerals are combined by addition, putting the largest unit at the left. Thus, MDCCCLXXXIII stands for 1883. When a smaller unit is placed to the left of a larger it is understood to be subtracted from it, and by this means very cumbersome combinations are sometimes avoided. Thus $IX = 9$, $XL = 40$, and $CM = 900$. For easier reading it is often the custom today to separate the groups of digits, the tens, the hundreds, the thousands, from each other by dots, thus:

M.CCCC.LXXXX.II

10. ARABIC NUMERALS. The system of numerals we use today originated in India. It consists of ten symbols, each of which receives a value of position as well as an absolute value. We are so familiar with this idea that we tend to overlook its merit and importance. The Arabs adopted the system in the 10th Century A.D. It reached Italy, via Spain, by the beginning of the 13th Century, and before long its superiority as a mathematical instrument was so obvious that the Roman numerals were discarded for all but a few decorative purposes. The first four symbols were originally somewhat similar to the Roman, the fingers being represented as horizontal rather than vertical strokes. In the margin we indicate the development of these signs into the symbols we know today. The five higher symbols, and the all-important zero, are of course quite different from anything in the Roman system.

Chapter 2. ROMAN LETTERS

1. STANDARD LETTERS. When Western Europe became the Roman Empire, and Latin its official language, Roman capitals became a standard alphabet. Before this there had been no standard letter systems among Semitic, Greek, or Latin peoples. This makes the first century of our era an important point in the history of our letters, for at that time all literate Europeans first thought of the letters they used in the same way. Before this we have a variety of shifting letter shapes everywhere different. After it we have an al-

most equal variety of shapes, but with a standard set of fixed exemplars behind it in all literate minds. These fixed standards remained because they were associated with the five-hundred-year rule of Europe by Rome, because everywhere they were visible in stone monuments, and because the barbaric centuries succeeding the Roman rule were intensely conservative, and in them men tended to look back rather than forward to good things. So today, when we think of A, we do not visualize a bull, or his head, or the Greek Alpha; we think of the Roman A either in its most primitive, or in its technically developed form.

2. EARLY LATIN CAPITALS. Before they were standardized, the letters of the earliest Latin inscriptions were so much like Greek letters that, though the words are Latin, the letters cannot be considered so. One of the early pieces of lettering that can be called Latin is the Scipio fragment. Here the P and the L are not very different from the Greek Pi and Lambda, and the inscription also shows its early date in the uncorrected forms of the skeletons. Notice the pure semicircles of the curved letters, and especially the tipped-back S. In later inscriptions the skeletons begin to be corrected. The ends of the stems begin to widen slightly, the serif develops, thick and thin strokes are differentiated, and it becomes apparent that these features are accepted as parts of the letters. Roman inscriptions show considerable differences in technical skill, but the development of the forms is steady and consistent.

3. DEVELOPED LATIN CAPITALS. In a good example of fully developed monumental letters, such as the inscription cut on the marble base of the Trajan Column (Plate XIX) early in the 2nd Century A.D., the skeletons are fully corrected, and materialized with serifs and thick and thin strokes. The tops of A, N, and M are pointed rather than serifed, a simpler solution from the stone-cutter's point of view. We have reason to believe that the normal procedure was for the designer to paint his inscription directly on the stone with a brush and then cut it with a chisel. A master brush-writer may have been employed to lay out inscriptions for the carvers, but it seems more likely that in most cases the carver was skillful enough to lay them out for himself.

CORNELIO L·F·SCIPIO
IDILES·COSOL·CESOR

AVGVSTVS
DRVSVS·CAESAR·AVG·F

95

ROGER BASTER
BLOCK MACKR
1687

JOHN STEVENS
1736

λ c/ιιι ʌ/ιι

(ιιλ ríνϵ

4. NEW ENGLAND PARALLEL. It is instructive to notice that the lettering on New England gravestones of the 17th and 18th Centuries follows a parallel development. We first find skeletons cut on stones, without serifs or difference in breadth of stroke. Gradually the same refinements develop, as the nature of the mind and the eye and the tools used are enabled to express themselves. At any time in the future, should similarly primitive conditions exist, we would expect to find these primitive letter shapes to reappear, and then gradually give place to forms of greater refinement.

5. MEMORIALS AND MEMORANDA. The letters of the Early Empire exist for us chiefly in such monuments as the Trajan Column, for these, whose purpose was to perpetuate memory, were made of hard and enduring materials. But only a fraction of the total amount of writing done at this time was thus memorial. The great mass of it was ephemeral—hastily written notes, lists, accounts, advertisements. The domestic scribbling of ordinary people who knew their letters was carried on carelessly then, as it is today.

6. WAX AND STYLUS. The common material for this rapid writing was the wooden tablet covered with a thin sheet of black wax. This smooth surface was scratched with a sharp, hard point—the stylus. The marks so made had not only the usual cursive qualities of compression, tilt, roundness, and the lengthening of verticals, but due to the tendency of the wax to cling to the stylus, the letters became separated into roughly vertical strokes. And due to the tendency of the point to turn in, they often acquired a backhanded tilt. This rapid letter-making on wax with a stylus produced an entirely different set of shapes from those of monumental letter-making with brush and chisel on stone, although at first the mental images were the same. The constant repetition of the muscular actions involved in making such marks, establishes, after a while, kinaesthetic images in the mind. When this is done, the image imposed on the material is no longer a visual one, badly adapted to the purpose and technique, but a kinaesthetic one, well adapted. When letters are written from kinaesthetic images, there is not much tendency to regard the results visually, or to compare

96

visually the cursive letters with their monumental prototypes. This is why such cursive scribbling is often accepted as a satisfactory method of communication, for considerable periods of time.

7. EYE AND HAND. The writing of the Ancient Romans comes down to us chiefly in these two extremely differentiated kinds, though the writers of them probably were not as conscious of the difference as we are. There were first the monumental letters, basically geometric and adapted to the mind, corrected to suit the eye, and adapted to the brush and chisel. Their shapes express the maximum of deference to the eye, and a minimum of deference to the hand. And there were also the cursive letters, originally written from the same images, but changed out of all recognition by the nature of the rapidly moving hand, and the nature of stylus and wax. Here there is practically no deference to the eye, and every concession is made to cursiveness.

8. THE THEME. But human nature is not satisfied with such extremes, visual or manual. Ultimately there will be a demand for a way of writing which conforms both to a visual standard of order, and a kinaesthetic standard of cursiveness. Visual forms may be suited to the hand, and cursive forms suited to the eye. From now on our story is a summary record of the never-ending struggle between the needs of the writing hand and of the reading eye, and a summary account of the shapes that have resulted from this struggle.

SENATVS
IMP·CAESARI
BDFGLOQX

ARMAVIRVMQVECANOTROIAE
QVIPRIMVSABORISITALIAMFATO
PROFVGVSLAVINIAQVEVENIT
LITORAMVLTVMILLEETTERRIS
IACTATVSETALTOVISVPERVM
SAEVAEMEMOREMIVNONISOB

ABCDEFGHILMNOPQRSTVXY·+

XIX. TRAJAN INSCRIPTION & SQUARE CAPITALS

98

PART B. THE MEDIEVAL WORLD

CHAPTER 1. MAJUSCULES

1. DESTRUCTION. Most of the lettering that has been preserved from the first centuries of our era consists either in monumental letters cut laboriously in stone, or cursives scratched hastily in wax. On the walls of the catacombs and the buried cities near Vesuvius, there has been discovered a good deal of brush-writing, formal in structure but executed freely. At Pompeii and in Egypt there have been unearthed many pen-written cursive papyrus manuscripts, more visually regular than the wax cursives. But with these exceptions the writing of the period, most of it presumably on papyrus, some of it on skins, has perished.

2. NEW MATERIALS. From the 5th Century onward, however, we have a growing number of examples. At this time writing upon parchment and vellum became so general that the codex or book was developed, which invention not only accounts for the preservation of the examples, but was itself a great stimulus to good writing. The papyrus scroll is the type of permanent literary record of the Pagan Roman world. The more enduring vellum codex is the type for the Christian Roman world. Our examples of pen-written descendants of the monumental Roman letters, therefore, date from the 5th Century. Because they occur chiefly in books they are called Book Hands.

3. NEW TOOLS. The new material made the book, but caused little change in the shape of the letters written in it. It was the new writing-tool, the wide-nibbed reed, that modified the letter shapes. Soon after, the quill began to be used for formal writing in books, superseding the narrow reed or small brush that had been used on papyrus.

4. NEW FORMS. The wide-pen letters which come to us from the 5th Century fall into two distinct classes—Capitals and Uncials. The skeletons of the former are of similar character to those of the monuments, but the Uncial skeletons include many new curves. Both Capitals and Uncials are called *Majuscules*, probably meaning *little big letters*—the small version, suitable for books, of letters carved large on monuments, or painted large on walls. Ma-

99

FELIXQVIPOTVITRERVMCOGNOSCERECAVSAS
ATQVEMETVSOMNISETINEXORABILEFATVM
SVBIECITPEDIBVSSTREPITVMQVEACHERONTIS
AVARIFORTVNATVSETILLEDEOSQVINOVIT
AGRESTISPANAQVESILVANVMQVESENEM
NYMPHASQVESORORESILIVMNONPOPVLI

ABCDEFGHILMNOPQRSTVXY   x

LITERAPYTHAGORAEDISCRIMINESEC
TABICORNIHUMANAEUITAESPECI
EMPRAEFERREUIDETURNAMUIA
UIRTUTISDEXTRUMPETITARDUA
CALLEMDIFFICILEMQUEADITUM
PRIMUMSPECTANTIBUSOFFERT

ABCDEFGHILMNOPQRSTUXYZ x

XX. RUSTIC CAPITALS & EARLY UNCIALS

100

juscules are in general written between two parallel lines. They were written larger or smaller for the sake of emphasis, but our notion of writing in two alphabets at once was unknown to any 5th Century penman.

5. SQUARE CAPITALS. There were two varieties of capitals, the *Square* and the *Rustic*. For the writing of classical poems and other serious works worthy of the most dignified treatment, pen letters were used that were as close to the monumental carved letters as was consistent with the natures of the hand and the pen. These were the Square capitals. The lower example in Plate XIX is a freely copied version of one of the earliest examples of this hand. The six following plates are also free modern copies of old manuscripts. Notice here the close spacing of the letters, and lack of extra space between words. One of the few skeleton changes is the vertical lengthening of F and L, probably to avoid, in a text without word space, confusion with E and I. Except for F and L, and the tail of Q, all the letters are contained within parallel lines. The transference of glyptic serifs to pen writing is another bond with the stone prototypes. Pen-made serifs ornament the ends of the thin strokes in such letters as A, V, N, and S, and the horizontals of E, F, L, and T. The only concessions to the needs of the writing hand seem to be the slight curvature in the diagonals in M and N, in the beard of G, and at the bottom of V. There is no lateral compression. The pen is held at a slight slant—about 20°, but is turned to almost 80°, to make the thin vertical of N.

6. RUSTIC CAPITALS. These letters can be written more rapidly than Square Capitals, but they are still a formal hand fit for dignified usages. They are written with an extreme pen slant— above 45°. For almost all the vertical strokes the pen is turned to beyond 70°. There is, therefore, a strong contrast of thicks and thins, with emphasis on the thicks. The skeletons are much modified in the interests of the hand. There is considerable lateral compression, especially noticeable in O. The cursive tendency to the omission of members shows in A, and to roundness in the beard of G and the bottom of V. The middle horizontal of E is unusually high, and H has a new shape. The loops of P and R are small.

101

SICINHUIUSMORTALITATIS
UIAPEREGRINANTESADOM
INOSIREDIREINPATRIAM
UOLUMUSUBIBEATIESSE
POSSIMUSUTENDUMEST
HOCMUNDONONFRUENDŪ

ABCDEFGHILMNOPQRSTU+

IN PRINCIPIO
CREAVIT·DEUS
CAELUM·ET·ERRAM
BDFGGHHKRQXZ·

XXI. LATE UNCIALS & VERSALS

102

Horizontal serifs are heavy, but there are none at the ends of horizontal strokes. As with the Square Capitals, F rises above E and L above I, but in general the letters are contained within the parallels.

7. EARLY UNCIALS. The Uncial is a Majuscule alphabet containing rounded forms of A, D, E, G, H, M, and V. It is written in the slanting pen position and combines a high degree of visual order with ease and rapidity of execution. Notice in the example that these letters, unlike Rustics, have not the cursive character of compression. They are written with a wide pen, held at an angle of less than 45°, from which position it is never shifted. There are no special manipulations. Such an alphabet as this we know to be early on account of the width of the pen stroke, the height of the middle bar of E, and the nearly vertical slope of the first and last strokes of M. In many ways these massive letters are the purest pen shapes that have ever been devised.

8. LATE UNCIALS. The skeleton difference between Uncials of the 5th and of the 8th Centuries is limited to three letters. In late Uncials the bar of E is lower, the first and last strokes of M more curved, and the tail of D nearly horizontal. The striking difference is in the pen slant, which is now practically straight, and in the accenting of thin strokes which the straight position requires. The pen is turned sideways for the thin verticals. Of the three kinds of Majuscules, Uncials became the favorite for books from the 5th to the 8th Centuries.

9. VERSALS. For special emphasis the scribe often wrote his Majuscules large, but when he wanted even more emphatic letters, for the beginnings of chapters, sections and *verses*, he made Built-ups, and these are appropriately called *Versals*. They were drawn with a quill following skeletons of both Capitals and Uncials, and reproducing the effects of both straight and slanting pen positions. The light, springy quality of the constructed strokes, the general thinness of the thicks, and the flat simple curves of the serifs, enable large Versals to be used with the small letters of text without overpowering them. The scribes usually took advantage of the need for filling in their Versals, to enrich their pages with colors both strong and gay. In about the 10th Century Versals reached their most per-

103

causaeueroquadripariamqu
arumunamquidemcausam
dicimusessesubstantiamun
amueromateriametsubiectu
tertiumautemdeprincip

abcdefʒhilmnopqrſtux   +

]ɥ principio erat uerbum 6ᴛ
uerbum erat apud deum 6ᴛ
deus erat uerbum hoc erat in
principio apud deum omnia
per ipsum facta 6ᴛ sine ipſo   +

abcodefʒhilmɥnopqrſtuxʒ

XXII. ROMAN & INSULAR HALF-UNCIALS

104

fect development, in England. They gave an opportunity for the greatest possible exuberance and fancy, and the making of them thus developed into *illumination*. Whether of the strictly two-dimensional, but amazingly fantastic type of the Book of Kells, or as it developed on the Continent in the late Middle Ages, into naturalistic representations of flowers, butterflies and three-dimensional landscapes, illumination has its origin in the imaginative elaboration of Versals.

CHAPTER 2. MINUSCULES

1. DEFINITION. Minuscules result from regularizing, to suit the eye, the cursive scrawlings of the stylus on wax. These scribblings show all the typically cursive qualities, and when they are adjusted to eye and pen, many of these qualities remain, especially roundness and the exaggeration of verticals. It is this last character that *defines* the minuscules as letters confined in three spaces between four horizontal lines.

2. ROMAN HALF–UNCIALS. The first Minuscules are called Half-Uncials. e, m, and t have Uncial skeletons, but the verticals of b, d, h, l, and s run far above the body space, and of f, g, p, and q drop far below it. Other skeleton changes appear in r, s, and g, the last having an angular form which it keeps for the next three centuries. Half-Uncials are written with the straight pen. The most important and regular of early half-uncial alphabets were those written in, or under the direct influence of, Rome. In the example notice the club-like ascenders. There are no special ending strokes. The writing is direct and simple, orderly and rapid,—evidently the work of a conscientious and forthright penman.

3. INSULAR HALF–UNCIALS. The book hands that developed in England and Ireland were Half-Uncials, and are well represented by the Irish Book of Kells, probably of the 8th Century. The verticals have triangular heads, and the ends of strokes are finished with distinction. Notice the pulled curves, and short ascenders and descenders. The variant of N, with its nearly horizontal diagonal, is characteristic, and persists in modern Irish lettering.

105

& uox citharedorum & musicorum & tibia
canentium & tuba non audietur in
te amplius & omnis artifex omnis
artis non invenietur in te amplius &
uox mole non audietur in te amplius

abcdEfghilmnopqrstuxy & x

Artifices si sunt in monasterio cum
omni humiltate faciant ipsas
artes si permiserit Abbas· Quod si
aliquis ex eis extollitur pro scientia
artis suae hic talis erigatur ab ipsa

abcdefghilmnopqrstuxz   x

XXIII. LOMBARDIC & CAROLINE MINUSCULE

4. NATIONAL BOOK HANDS. While the Insular hands were developing in isolation, the disunity and confusion of political conditions on the continent expressed themselves in a wilderness of provincial and national book hands, each with its own local oddities, and all more or less degenerate. All these hands were minuscules. The best of them was the Lombardic of Italy, which developed an interesting zigzag pattern, which later became so pronounced as to earn the name of *broken Lombardic*. Our example is from the late 11th Century. Notice the zigzag quality, and the peculiar skeletons of A, E, R, and especially T. The ascenders are long and clubbed, the pen slant about 45°, and, as in Kells, there is a tendency to word division.

5. CAROLINE MINUSCULE. The political reforms of Charlemagne were accompanied by cultural reforms, an important part of which was the work of calligraphic scholars, headed by Alcuin of York, at Tours in France. These men set to work, late in the 8th Century, and after a long and careful study of calligraphy to that date, produced a new hand, the standard book hand for the Carolingian Empire. In this alphabet the best characters of the various national minuscule hands were retained, and their local oddities and illogicalities purged away. Cursive requirements were carefully studied, and a new set of mental patterns based on them, established and standardized. The example shows the breadth and sweep which this hand derived from the half-uncials that preceded it. It shows in the easy strokes of r and s, and in the width of the curves of m and a. The flat-headed G comes from Lombardic and other national alphabets, but such odd shapes as the insular alternative N, and the Lombardic E, R, and T have been abandoned. The alphabet has the orderliness of the insular hands and the pen slant of the national hands, being in our example less than 45°. The stroke endings are simple but entirely adequate. There is a definite spacing between words. An entirely new feature is the slight tilt of the letters themselves to the right. This is a new concession to cursiveness, and one of the elements in the admirable balance which this hand achieves, between the kinaesthetic and the visual.

Vanitas est diligere.quod cum omni celeritate transit et illuc non festinare,ubi sempiternum gaudium manet. Memento illius frequenter proverbii; quia non satiatur oculus visu, nec auris impletur auditu. De Imitatione Christi.

abcdefghiklmnopqrstuvxyz Ecclesiastes 1-8 x

Propter quae proprie et communiter decet juste considerantes ad omnes deos et homines eum qui vitam habet et multu ad suam uxorem et filios et parentes.
Aristotiles Oeconomica.

abcdefg hijklmnopqrstuvxyz·oz·   x

XXIV. NORTHERN & SOUTHERN GOTHIC

6. NORTHERN GOTHIC. With the death of Charlemagne, Christendom, though still culturally one, became again politically many. The calligraphic symbol of unity maintained itself longer than that which it symbolized, but eventually it also yielded to the pressure of national and local preferences, and the minuscule book hands began to diversify geographically once more. These diversified descendants of the Caroline Minuscule are the characteristic book hands of the High Middle Ages. These fell into two general groups, a northern and a southern. England, the Low Countries, northern France and Germany represent the North. Here the tendency to emphasize verticals produced the angular black letter, where the body of the text consists of little but vertical strokes, connected in various ways with hair lines so as to be legible as letters. Such writing has been likened to a wooden pale fence, and to relieve the monotony of the repeated verticals the scribes allowed themselves the greatest freedom in the exuberance with which they treated their initial letters. From the 9th to the 15th Century the tendency of northern Gothic was thus to greater and greater angularity and monotony in the minuscules, combined with increasing playfulness and floridity in the capitals. In six centuries the Caroline Minuscule had developed into the hand of our example, which is an extreme example neither of monotony in the minuscules, nor of exuberance in the capitals. The pen slant is less than 45°, and the words are now separated by still more definite spaces.

7. SOUTHERN GOTHIC. The corresponding southern group, comprising southern France, Spain and Italy, developed during the same period a different black letter, rounded rather than angular, and with less contrast between small letters and capitals. In the minuscules, the straight strokes remain vertical, as in m and n, but in such letters as b, o, and s the curved strokes remain full curves, and are not translated into rigid palings as they were in the North. There is, therefore, much more contrast as well as legibility in the text, and a correspondingly lesser need for the relief of flourished capitals. The pen slant is the same as for the northern Gothic.

IS·DEMVM·MIHI·VIVERE·ATQ3
frui anima uidetur, qui, aliquo
negotio intentus, praeclari facinoris
aut artis bonae famam quaerit.
ABCDEFGHILMNOPQRSTVX ~

abcdefghilmnopqrfstux · · ✕

Che impofsibile mi pare che la sua
operazione sia nelle piu cose altro che
dolce, conciofsiacosachè i nomi seguitano
le nominate cose, siccome è scritto:
Nomina sunt consequentia rerum.

abcdefghilmno pqr fstuz ✕

XXV. HUMANISTIC MINUSCULE & ITALIC

8. HUMANISTIC MINUSCULE. By the 15th Century, any-thing with a Gothic or northern flavor about it smacked to sophisti-cated people of the barbarism of the Middle Ages that were passing, and the scholarly hand was cleared of all the characteristics of black letter. Our example represents the Italian book hand of the early Renaissance. Notice the similarity and difference of the capi-tals from Square Capitals. The skeletons are the same but these are written not with so straight a pen, but with a slant of more than 30°. The ascenders and descenders are ended in triangular heads. The words are divided by full spaces, and by marks of punctuation.

9. ITALIC. The lower example shows the famous Italic hand of the next century. It differs from the Humanistic minuscule in its greater cursiveness. The letters are laterally compressed, the as-cenders and descenders are long, the strokes which had been verti-cal are tilted to the right about 5°, and the axes of the loops are sloped at about 15°. The pen slant is about 45°. Except on the ends of ascenders and descenders there are no serifs. The hand is clear and may be written fairly rapidly. Like the northern black letter, with which it corresponds in several ways, the lateral compression gives great evenness of color to the page, though it does not in itself increase legibility. Notice that the capitals are not tilted. The 16th Century scribes used the same vertical capitals with both Humanistic and Italic minuscules.

10. ENGLAND. The insular half-uncial developed in England into a rounded slanting pen hand which, because Alcuin was an Englishman, had some influence on the Caroline minuscule. But here, as in other northern countries, the reformed minuscule de-veloped into an angular black letter, in which all late Medieval English manuscripts were written. It was not until the press had been established in England that these angular letters were aban-doned for general use in favor of the rounded types developed in Italy. The typographic term *Old English* means the black letter which was given up. The traditional familiarity of rounded pre-Caroline forms may be partly responsible for the abandon-ment of black letter by England, so long before the other northern countries.

111

Northern gothic
or Blackletter?

ABCDEFG
HIJKLMN
OPQRST
VVWXYZ

abcdefghijklmn
opqrstuvwxyz

XXVI. BLACKLETTER

Southern or
Round gothic
ABCDEFG
HIJKLMN
OPQRST
UVWXYZ

abcdefghijlm
nopqrstuvxyz

XXVII. ROUND GOTHIC

113

ABCDEF
GHIJKL
MNOPQ
RSTUV
WXYZ·
CAPITALS

XXVIII. CAPITALS

114

abcdefg
hijklmn
opqrstu
vwxyz 1 2
3456789·
humanist

XXIX. SMALL LETTERS

115

XXX. ITALIC CAPITALS

Chancery Italic

abcdefgghij
klmnopqqrs
ſtuvwxyyz.

Cursive·Hands

XXXI. ITALIC SMALL

11. THE FINAL HANDS. The last four hands that we have discussed fall into two general classes, the gothic and the classic. These hands are the calligraphic legacy of the Middle Ages to the modern world. It is these which the first printers copied, and it is adaptations of these which calligraphers use today. For convenience in the study of these important forms, we show them written in a larger size in Plates XXVI to XXXII.

12. PRINTING. The establishment of the press is one of the historic facts that brought the Middle Ages to an end. For the historian of calligraphy it is the chief fact. By it the development of letter forms, some of which we indicate in the margin, was arrested. The letters in the right-hand columns are quite similar to those we use today. But for our purpose it has another importance. The establishment of the corrected skeleton and the cutting of this on enduring stone monuments had fixed the Roman Capital once and for all in the minds of western men as an alphabet in its own right. The development of the Caroline minuscule, as the cultural instrument of the New Empire, established the small letter in a perfect form in the minds of literate European men. So the establishment of the printing press defined permanently the relations of these two alphabets to each other. The tendency had been in the air for centuries, but the necessity of the typographer to decide definitely what type he was going to use, and how he was going to use it, brought the matter to a decision. No longer could calligraphic compromises be made. The convention was established of using the more dignified and monumental alphabet for the most dignified and monumental uses, and the more informal and cursive alphabet for the rest. Thus the beginning, the middle, and the end of the Medieval Period, mark the establishment of the three conventions which govern our modern writing—the capital, the small letter, and the relation between them.

118

PART C. THE MODERN WORLD

CHAPTER 1. WRITING AND CARVING

1. INFORMAL HANDS. The Medieval World closes with the supplanting of the scriptorium by the press as the producer of books. After the establishment of presses it was cheaper to print books than to write them, but writing nevertheless continued. At first only the most important pieces of literature were produced by the new method. All through the Middle Ages people had written cursive and informal scripts for letters, accounts, announcements, deeds, chancery records,—all the various uses for which today we are apt to employ the typewriter. Now when books were no longer written, these less formal hands continued as before. But with the passage of time the traditional memory of the formal letter shapes grew dim, and their place in the mind was taken by the shapes of types. The writers of informal hands had no longer behind them the example and discipline of the work of the professional scribes.

2. COPY BOOKS. For this, among other reasons, the printed copy book came into existence. People needed help to maintain good calligraphic standards. At about the same time the writing tool also changed. Instead of a short, stiff quill cut to a chisel edge, filled not dipped, and used at a desk of steep inclination, a long, flexible quill came into use, cut to a point, with a long slit, the pen being dipped rather than filled, and the inclination of the desk much reduced. With such a pen, variations of pressure give a strong difference of breadth of stroke, which is independent of linear direction. The use of such a quill is also responsible for the exuberant calligraphic ornament with which these copy books were so often enriched. Both the letters and the unilinear adornments were at first reproduced with woodcuts, of which the upper reproduction is an example; but later the copperplate was more often used, the burin being admirably adapted to the reproduction of delicate curves of varying weight. The lower two illustrations are reproduced from copper engravings.

3. DEGENERATION. Before printing, the cursive hands were the least formal of written letters. Now, the copy book cursives are the most formal, and the less formal have moved still further in the

119

kinaesthetic direction, or, as we say, degenerated into scribble. The substitution of flexible steel nibs for pointed quills, at the time of the Industrial Revolution, does not seem to have caused much change. The chief causes of the decay of handwriting seem to have been the substitution of typographic for calligraphic standards in literate people's minds, and the neglect of stroke sequence. But whatever were the causes, it is a fact that writing did degenerate—rapidly toward the end of the 19th Century and thereafter.

4. REFORM. There were many attempts to check the lapse into scrawling, almost all ineffectual because not based on a knowledge of the principles of normal lettering. Perhaps the first really constructive reformer was William Morris, who tackled the problem from the point of view of the craftsman, the student of techniques. Maunde Thompson's work was perhaps equally important, his approach being the more theoretical one of the student of Palaeography. The practical discoveries of Morris and the scholarship of Thompson bore fruit in the really effective work of a third Englishman, Edward Johnston, and the German, Rudolph Koch. Johnston and Koch stand at the heads of the schools of calligraphic reform in their respective countries. Each has a large number of followers, and, as far as we know, serious attempts at restoration of good writing in other countries are all indebted for their inspiration in one way or another to either Johnston or Koch.

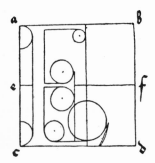

5. RENAISSANCE FORMULAE. The modern history of carved letters has been generally parallel to that of the written. It was characteristic of the Renaissance designers—eager to reproduce the beauty of ancient letters, anxious to get back to first principles, and yet contemptuous of an unfashionable philosophy by means of which they would have been able to reach these first principles—that they attempted to formulate a set of mechanical rules. By means of these they hoped that true Roman capitals could be drawn by means of straight edge and compass. These men saw that geometry played a part in the formation of capitals, but they were ignorant as to just what that part was. Albrecht Dürer, Sebastian Serlio, Geoffrey Tory, and Leonardo da Vinci were among the most notable artists who made this attempt. The designs they pro-

120

Apprentice that he the Master will pay to the Ap
during the first year nothing during the second year ti
the third year the sum of fifteen shillings weekly dur
pound weekly during the fifth year the sum of one po
Father and the Apprentice do and each of them doth h
the absence from work of the Apprentice on account of
account of military service or for any cause for which t
these said wages shall cease until the return to work of t
the Master and the Father doth hereby covenant with
incapacity from illness or otherwise of the Master to
or of his death or of the incapacity from illness or of
consecutive months or of the death of the Apprenti
of the said term thereupon these presents shall cease a
doth hereby covenant with the Father and the App
said term of service or on the sooner determination of
presents shall be handed over to the Apprentice or ti
service endorsed thereon In Witness whereof

XXXII. PORTION OF SEMI–FORMAL MS.
BY EDWARD JOHNSTON

121

duced, based as they were on a careful study of classical originals, are fairly satisfactory under certain conditions—those of the monuments which they copied. But because letters have technical and functional as well as imaginative causes, their designs, even under the most favorable conditions, failed to capture the true spirit of the classical inscriptions. And when applied to purposes and techniques of more various sorts, the resulting shapes were absurd.

6. NEW ENGLAND GRAVESTONES. The Renaissance did not seriously affect the arts of North America until the beginning of the 18th Century. For example 17th Century colonial architecture is basically Gothic and Medieval. The type of framing which resulted in the overhanging upper storey, the casement window with diamond panes, and the great central *tulip* chimney were elements in the Medieval building tradition. So the letters cut on early gravestones are unaffected by the theories of the great Renaissance designers. Our old graveyards bear witness to the enormous amount of letter-cutting in colonial America, and much of this was very distinguished. The excellence of the best American work was due to the fact that these humble masons were not derivative as the Renaissance masters had been. They reproduced in stone the simple *ideas* of letters which were in their heads, not the *effects* of letters on antique monuments. And they were practical stone-cutters themselves, and they knew what Dürer and da Vinci did not know, the true meaning of the technical qualities of letters.

7. DEGENERATION AND REFORM. In Europe and America the degeneration of written letters in the 19th Century was paralleled by a degeneration of carved letters. The reaction to this degeneracy was inevitable, but because, in modern times, the artistic reformer has been seldom a man of stone and chisels, it came later than in other techniques. It was not until the 20th Century that Eric Gill, much influenced by the calligraphic reforms of Johnston, but himself a stone-cutter, initiated the long awaited reformation of Glyptic letters. A man of original and philosophic mind, he was as little attracted by derivatism as by naturalism, and was realistic enough to be willing to think of stone-cut letters in terms of cutting and stones, as well as in terms of imagination and legibility.

122

ABC
DEFGHIJK
abcdefghijklmn
LMNOPQR
opqrstuvwxyz
STUVWXY
123456789&
Z

XXXIII. RUBBING OF A STONE CUT BY ERIC GILL

iacob. Surge·⁊
ibi: facq̃ altare
quãto fugîebas
uero conuocata

Uita data é vrēd
Mutua:neccerta

Illudq̃ cui equo:
ac ſerio habitu &

r um pius Oeagrij,
A dmonita genitrice refert,
I nachiosq; uias, pelaguq;

Quouſque tandem
abutere, Catilina,

1. INVENTION. The first types were close imitations of the shapes of the best book hands of their day and locality. Johannes Gutenberg devised and used an angular northern black letter type, Erhard Ratdolt, a round southern black letter. Nicolas Jenson made a typographic version of the humanistic hand, which we now call Roman upper and lower case; and Aldus Manutius, an Italic. These were the principal classes of type, through the use of which the Medieval chapter of the history of European letters was brought to a close. With some changes, they are the types which we use today.

2. CONTRADICTION. These first types are among the best that have been designed. They were produced as close imitations, sometimes definitely fraudulent, of the contemporary book hands. This seeming contradiction—that an imitation of the shapes of one technique by another should produce good and beautiful results—is understandable when we consider, first, that the designers of the types were not only the cutters of the punches, but also the printers who used the type itself. There was the maximum of knowledge of technique and control over technical factors. And, second, these first printers and type designers were themselves trained calligraphers, and therefore thoroughly competent to solve, as far as they can be solved in type, the problems of spacing and arrangement upon which legibility depends. The history of the development of typography in the next few centuries is the reversal of both these tendencies. There is a progressive improvement, in that printed letters slowly become less thought of as copies of written letters, and more as shapes in their own right. Types properly become less calligraphic. But there is also a progressive movement away from well-proportioned skeletons, and from the traditional solutions to the problem of the distribution of weight.

3. OLD FACE. All the earlier adaptations of the types of Jenson and Aldus are known as Old Face types. One of the most notable of the English punch cutters was William Caslon, a gunsmith. His training in the making of tiny steel shapes with files and punches fitted him technically for his work as a type designer. His type kept

124

the superficial character of the older forms, but gave them a more regular geometric structure. Caslon old style is still used by many of our presses.

4. MODERN FACE. A further step in the direction of mechanical regularity was taken by Giambattista Bodoni. The letters he produced were typographic rather than calligraphic. They were designed not as letters written with a pen, but as letters constructed by drawing. The thicks and thins are based on the straight pen position, but in a very simplified and mechanical relationship to one another. The thicks are not too heavy, but the thins and serifs tend to become mere hair lines. This type was inspired by a romantic view of the classic past. The followers of Bodoni did not avoid the dangers inherent in the construction of Built-ups. In the 19th Century an exaggerated thickness of the thicks was added to the wiriness of the thins. The skeletons were distorted both by lateral extension and compression. These *fat-faced* types, although definitely debased, nevertheless became very popular. While satisfactory enough in neo-classic marble inscriptions on account of the whiteness of the material, they were ill suited to the bold contrast of black and white in print.

5. DEGENERATION. In general, the types of the 19th Century lapsed so far from their kind—from the reasons which letters have for existence—that they are properly called degenerate. Shapes change as causes change, and any distortion is legitimate and acceptable when it is the effect of causes which are themselves part of the good life of the people who produce them. But a restless love of change for its own sake is not a sign of a stable society nor a happy people, and is not a legitimate cause for such changes as were made in our printed letters in the 19th Century. The results were not long satisfying, and like the fancifulness and illegibility of the pre-Caroline book hands, they bred a reaction and a reform. Men of two kinds, with quite different points of view, have sought to solve the problem of the degeneracy of types. The first group are those that reject, and the second those that accept, the Industrial Revolution and the changes that it has wrought in the relations of men.

BODONI
of Parma

FAT FACE
EXTENDED
CONDENSED

DEROME,
AMERICAN
CORDOVA,

125

6. TRADITIONALISTS. William Morris was enraged at the misery, the falsehood, and the ugliness of the England of the early industrial period. He believed that industrialism was bad because he saw its oppression of man by man, putting instruments of economic tyranny into the hands of those insufficiently trained in will and intellect to use them wisely or mercifully. He, therefore, devoted his life to the effort to restore men to a (perhaps imaginary) condition of self-dependence and freedom. His reforms of printed types are the reflection of this general point of view. His method was to disregard the conditions of industrial production around him, and to study older letter forms. Although an enthusiastic admirer of Medieval manuscripts, and an indefatigable penman, he apparently made little analysis of calligraphic forms, but contented himself with adapting early types, particularly that of Jenson, and the southern black letter. His Roman lower case types were heavier than his models, and therefore more Gothic. He disliked the excessive thicks and thins, and lateral compression of contemporary types, but although he aimed at legibility, he did not completely achieve it. He did not know enough either about the pen or the press. His method was derivative rather than analytical. But his principle of action was to fit the tool to the thing he wanted to produce. In general the reform of the less extreme traditionalists has been to the revival of the Old Face types.

7. INDUSTRIALISTS. The other group accept industrialism, as a present fact, and as a permanent necessity. They accept the mechanization of life, the division of men into designers on the one hand, and executors of the projects of designers on the other, but they hope to improve the quality of the products of industrialism by a study of its nature, and a fitting of the product to the instrument that is to produce it. They reject calligraphy as having nothing to do with the contemporary design problem, but study the conditions of mechanical production. This leads them to very simple shapes, the kind mechanism can best reproduce, and they have designed some letters like the earliest Latin inscriptions. Modern *sans-serifs* are the typical product of this school. Paul Renner's Futura is probably its most perfect example. The Bauhaus has

in golde, syluer and
themperour, and the
hys helme whan he

hous of Troye
for oon aduersite

FUTURA
BLACK
MEDIUM

been their most characteristic center. Herbert Bayer represents the extremists of the group, interested not only in producing something good, but also something definitely new and unlike what has been done before. An example of this pursuit of novelty is the suppression of the Capital. There seems no reason to believe that any lettering factor as useful as the Capital will be lightly abandoned by society in general. The Middle Ages reduced the importance of the Capital, and the early 19th Century tried to abolish it, but without success. Like punctuation, it is important to the conveying of exact thought, and while exact communication is valued, will probably not be abandoned. If we keep the Capital, we shall do so not because it is familiar, but because it is legible.

AFTERWORD

THERE are those who think of themselves self-consciously as designers of letters—*artists*. There are simpler people who satisfy themselves with giving their customers what they are asked for. And there are the mass of us—scribbling a momentary record, or a note to a friend. All make letters.

Many of these have acquired an amazing degree of manual dexterity and technical knowledge,—the engraver of silver with his burins, the sign-writer with his long flexible brush, the stone-cutter with his chisel, the bender of glass tubes for neon signs. When occasionally the skillful hands of such men are guided by good mental images, we get the most beautiful results. We sometimes see brush-written capitals in the windows of shops and restaurants that compare favorably with wall-writing of the Romans; or engraving in silver as good as anything from the past. But these are the exceptions. The great mass of the letters produced by these skillful hands are debased and vulgar. And when an art museum pays for such lettering, and exhibits it to the public, it is no less degenerate.

But when we see beautiful letters executed today it is because a dextrous hand has been guided by an informed mind. Our contemporary world does not lack technical knowledge and trained hands as much as it lacks formal knowledge and trained imaginations. If sign-writers, benders of neon tubes, and designers of Built-ups could see good forms in their heads, they could make perfect letters, for they already have all the dexterity needful.

For the man who is satisfied with what he sees about
128

him—in newspapers, on shop-fronts, on tombstones, or carved on the façades of important buildings, there is no problem. This book is written for those who are not so satisfied, either with the letters they see made by others, or with those they see made by themselves, but who have neither the leisure nor the opportunities to study a subject so intricate.

Letters exist to serve men. If we make them to be our servants, they might as well be good ones. The authors hope that this book will help those who are seriously interested, to make the letters they are responsible for, good. These cannot be good letters—legible—unless they are also true—what they purport to be. And they cannot be beautiful—pleasing to the mind—unless they are both good and true.

BIBLIOGRAPHY

CHAPELL, WARREN
   The Anatomy of Lettering. *Loring & Mussey, New York.*
   An excellent brief discussion.

DEGERING, HERMAN
   Lettering. 240 Plates. *Ernest Benn, Ltd., London, 1929.*
   Many good photographs of historic forms.

DWIGGINS, W. A.
   Layout in Advertising. *Harper & Brothers, New York.*
   A capable handbook for commercial work.

GILL, ERIC
   Typography. *Sheed & Ward, New York.*
   A brief, philosophic discussion.

HEWITT, GRAILY
   Lettering. *J. B. Lippincott, Philadelphia.* (*New Art Library.*)
   Contains the best technical advice on gilding in illumination.

HOFFMAN, HERBERT (*Editor*)
   Modern Lettering. *William Helburn, New York.*
   A comprehensive collection of contemporary examples.

HOLME, C. G. (*Editor*)
   Lettering of Today. *Studio Publications, Inc., New York.*
   Encouraging examples of modern writing and construction.

HÜBNER, ÆMILIUS
   Exempla Scripturae Epigraphicae Latinae. *Berlin, 1885.*
   Accurate outline scale drawings of Roman inscriptions.

JOHNSTON, EDWARD and GILL, ERIC
   Writing and Illuminating and Lettering. *Sir Isaac Pitman & Sons, Ltd., London.*
   The classical treatise on its subject. The section on Illumination treats fully of ornament and the use of color.

   Manuscript and Inscription Letters.
   Portfolio with 16 plates by the same masters.

SIMONS, ANNA
   Titel und Initialen. *The Bremmer Press, Munich, 1926.*
   A portfolio of this artist's work, including many fine Built-ups.

BIBLIOGRAPHY

THOMPSON, Sir Edward Maunde

An Introduction to Greek and Latin Palaeography. *The Clarendon Press, Oxford, 1912.*

The history of early manuscripts, with many illustrations.

UPDIKE, Daniel Berkeley

Printing Types, Their History, Forms and Use. *Harvard University Press, Cambridge, Massachusetts, 1937. 2 vols.*

The standard work on its subject.

YEE, Chiang

Chinese Calligraphy. *Methuen & Co., Ltd., London.*

An illuminating discussion of Far Eastern calligraphy showing interesting parallels in underlying principle.

These works will be valuable for the student, but he should neglect no opportunity to study original manuscripts, carved inscriptions and early writing books, as well. And, above all, pen and chisel in hand, he should practice.

131

INDEX

132

INDEX

G

geometry, 8
Gill, Eric, 122, 123; Pl. XXXIII, 123
glyptic,
 definition of, 10; letters, 74, 122
Gothic, 118
 Northern, 109, 111, 118, 124, Pl.
 XXIV, 108, Pl. XXVI, 112; Southern, 109, 124, Pl. XXIV, 108, Pl.
 XXVII, 113
graphic,
 definition of, 10; plain, 65
gravestones, 96, 122
Gutenberg, Johannes, 124

H

half-uncials, 105, Pl. XXII, 104
hand, 16, 47, 49, 97,
 position of, in writing, 47
humanistic minuscule, 111, Pl. XXV,
 110, Pl. XXIX, 115

I

image,
 consciousness of, 16; definition of, in
 art, 4; formal, 4; insight, 25; simplicity of, 13; ultimacy of, 14
imagination,
 definition of, 4–5
incising,
 materials and tools, 71–73, Pl. XIX,
 98, Pl. XXXIII, 123; technique,
 73–77, 95
inclination,
 of board, 46
ink, 41
italics,
 35, 38, 58, 111, Pl. V, 37; capitals,
 Pl. XI, 57; Pl. XXX, 116; small,
 Pl. X, 56; Pl. XXV, 110; Pl. XXXI,
 117

J

Jenson, Nicholas, 124
Johnston, Edward, 120–122; Pl.
 XXXII, 121

K

kinaesthesis, 4, 5, 18, 33, 45, 46, 49, 50
Koch, Rudolph, 120

L

layout,
 brush, on stone, 74; full size, 40; on
 paper, 75
legibility, 78–81
letters,
 ancient, 91–97; built-up, 65–69; constructed, 64–69; cut, 77; drawn, 64–
 69; majuscule, 99–105; marked,
 39–40; medieval, 98–118; minuscule,
 105–118; modern, 119–121; plain,
 65–67, 69–70, 74; skeleton, 25–38;
 slanting pen, 50–58; straight pen,
 58–64; use of, 78–88; written, 41–64
ligatures, 64, 80
linear,
 diversity, 29; figures, 28, Pl. I, 26;
 illegibility, 29; legibility, 29; letters,
 40; uniformity, 29
lines,
 definition of, in lettering, 9; and
 letter size, 86; and planes, 28; and
 surfaces, 77; as unit, 82-83
lombardic minuscule,
 107, Pl. XXIII, 106

M

majuscules, 99–105
 rustic capitals, 101, Pl. XX, 100;
 square capitals, 101, Pl. XIX, 98;
 uncials, early, 103, Pl. XX, 100;
 uncials late, 103, Pl. XXI, 102;
 versals, 103, Pl. XXI, 102 (*See*
 capitals, round forms)

REPRODUCED FOR McGRAW-HILL BOOK COMPANY, NEW YORK
FROM TYPE SET BY D. B. UPDIKE, THE MERRYMOUNT PRESS,
BOSTON, IN THE MONTH OF MAY 1940.
REVISIONS SET BY THE PLIMPTON PRESS, NORWOOD, MASS.
PRINTED BY ROBERT TELLER SONS & DORNER OFFSET CO., N. Y.